Making Values *Real*

ENDORSEMENTS

Dr Arnold Smit's passion for ethical leadership and values is truly inspiring. This book, Making Values Real brings this passion to life, offering pragmatic insights, real-life examples, and tools to help leaders navigate ethical dilemmas with confidence. His work and focus on actionable strategies align with UONGOZI Institute's mission — to inspire and equip leaders with the tools for inclusive and sustainable leadership. It is an essential resource for any leader committed to making values a guiding force in their decisions and actions.

Emmanuel Tessua, Acting Director of Executive Education, UONGOZI Institute, Tanzania

This is a transformative must-read for anyone aspiring to sharpen their efforts in values-led leadership and how to deeply integrate values into their daily leadership practices. This book is not a "theoretical quest", but an actionable guide with illustrations, reflections, tool, tips and exercises that will inspire and deepen commitment to making our values real.

I love the powerful analogy of "yeast" as an essential ingredient in baking, as being similar to values being pivotal to effective leadership. The "yeast effect" being a beautiful metaphor for the catalytic impact yeast has on the texture, the experience, the flavour, and the nourishment of the bread. Just so, values of respect, integrity, empathy, adaptability, ethics, accountability and impact are vital to the role of leadership.

Inspired by values to make a difference.

Dr Shirley Zinn, Chair and Independent Non-Executive Board Director: Sanlam, MTN (SA), VNA, Spur Corporation and Spar Group

Making Values Real blends the theory of values-based leadership with practical application, empowering leaders and managers to integrate values effectively into their daily practices. In addition to providing a sound theoretical guide, the engaging writing style, practical examples, and reflective exercises ensure that anyone can grasp and apply the concepts with ease. This book is a valuable resource for those looking to cultivate principled workplace cultures and essential reading for anyone committed to growing as a values-based leader and fostering an environment of integrity, trust, and respect within their organisations.

Prof Mias de Klerk, Professor in Leadership and Organisational Behaviour, Editor-in-Chief: South African Journal of Business Management, Director: Centre for Responsible Leadership Studies (Africa), Stellenbosch Business School

This book represents a valuable contribution to the topic of values-based leadership. Managing from a values-based perspective is integral to leading ethically with integrity and transparency. Ample frameworks and examples make the book useful for practice grounded in sound theoretical structures.

Prof Marius Ungerer, Emeritus Professor, Academic area: Strategic Management and Leadership, Stellenbosch Business School

Values have enormous transformative power in organisations and individuals. However, unlocking the transformative potential of values requires skill and wisdom. Making Values Real offers valuable insights born out of real-life experiences that Arnold Smit acquired in his extensive experience of working with organisations. The metaphor of yeast that he employs in the sub-title of the book is apt as it signifies how values can transform people and organisations. Baking with yeast is both a science and an art. This book is rich in both these ingredients.

Prof Deon Rossouw, Former CEO of The Ethics Institute,
Extraordinary Professor in Business Ethics,
Founding President of the Business Ethics Network of Africa

I have had the privilege to know and work with Professor Arnold Smit during several workshops on values-based leadership over time. It is while critically engaging with health professionals from heterogenous backgrounds in workshops over a few days that their true values in leadership became very clear. Professor Smit's vast experience and skills in evoking people's values and emotions behind their professional practice has made him an authority on this subject. This book offers a valuable resource for people who are serious about gaining skills to work out their values and ethics in everyday practice.

Louis Jenkins, Professor of Family Medicine, Stellenbosch University, Honorary associate professor, Cape Town University

What you are holding in your hands is not simply a collection of words with meanings; it is a distillation of Arnold's lifelong quest for authentic living. Arnold has poured himself fully into every page of this book, sharing the questions he wrestles with daily in his own life. In doing so, he demonstrates that living life is a hopeful quest inspired by the belief in a better and healthier world. Arnold does not shy away from admitting that we will, many times, get it wrong, and at such times, confrontation becomes necessary. Here, Arnold provides us with very helpful guidelines, tools, and even stories to support our quest for making values real. This book is like the greater honey guide bird, which, in a symbiotic relationship with the honey gatherers, leads them to the beehive. Once you reach the hive, the onus is on you regarding what to do next with the guide that led you there, the large deposits of honey and whether future generations will be equally rewarded because you thought about them.

Samuel Gikaru Njenga, Management and Leadership Consultant and Director of Systems Thinking Africa

First published in 2025.

ISBN: 978-1-991272-25-6 (Printed)
eISBN: 978-1-991272-26-3 (PDF eBook)

Published by KR Publishing

Tel: (011) 706-6009
E-mail: orders@knowres.co.za
Website: www.kr.co.za

Typesetting, layout and design: Cia Joubert, cia@knowres.co.za
Cover design: Marlene De Lorme, marlene@knowres.co.za
Editing & proofreading: KR Publishing Team
Project management: Cia Joubert, cia@knowres.co.za

Focus on the Yeast Effect

A Practical Guide to Living, Leading and Building Relationships Through Values

Arnold Smit

2025

VALUES

TABLE OF CONTENTS

FOREWORD

By Mary C. Gentile PhD
Creator/Director, Giving Voice to Values

As I sat down to read Arnold Smit's book on *Making Values Real*, I anticipated it would be insightful and practical, with many lessons for anyone who works in and/or with organisations. But what I was not expecting was how personally inspiring the book would be. My friendship and colleagueship with Arnold go back many years to our first meeting at Stellenbosch Business School in Cape Town, South Africa. We both worked in executive and graduate business education, but I didn't know the ways in which his life's work would intersect with my own and how his personal commitment to promoting responsible and values-driven organisational practice would serve to reinforce and amplify my own aspirations.

To understand why *Making Values Real* had this impact, it is useful to understand my own path. I have spent most of my professional life trying to find more effective and impactful ways to educate, train and inspire organisational leaders and other professionals to voice and act on their values more often and more effectively. This purpose grew out of my frustration with the traditional ways that organisational ethics were taught in schools and promoted in businesses and other organisations. The focus tended to be on teaching the "rules" but without an emphasis on any practical "tools" on teaching awareness and analysis but not action; on ethical decision-making, but not on implementation. I call this the "preach and pretend" method; we will preach to learners about what is right and then pretend that they can or will do it.

Because of this frustration, I experienced what I call a "crisis of faith" earlier in my career, feeling that my work was at best futile and, at worst, hypocritical. Out of this crisis grew my own conviction that efforts to educate, train and support practitioners and professionals would require a different approach, an approach that involved a recognition that values conflicts are the rule rather than the exception; that there are many ways to act on our values and that we can play to our own personal strengths; and importantly, that pre-scripting, rehearsal and peer coaching are critical components to building the "Moral Muscle Memory" to effectively voice these values.

I had the honour of sharing my thinking with Arnold at a convening of business educators from across Africa and one of my most enduring memories of that gathering was Arnold's reaction. Clearly our thinking and approaches were in sync. It meant the world to me at that time, many years ago, that he so reinforced my thinking and early efforts in this direction.

But now, after reading *Making Values Real,* I am encouraged and inspired to see the lessons and insights Arnold has developed and the impact he has had in taking this commitment to supporting values-driven action into the many organisations where he has shared it. In his book, Arnold is exceedingly generous, sharing the foundational thinking and ideas behind his approach; guiding principles for designing and implementing programs for values-driven leadership development; as well as a plethora of practical tools and exercises for building self-awareness and crafting and rehearsing scripts and action plans for addressing organisational and individual values conflicts successfully.

One of the most powerful aspects of Smit's approach is his emphasis upon "communicative action," the power of using words to not only move individuals and organisations but to, in effect, create new realities that make ethical action not only possible but much more likely. But this powerful use of language requires reflection, analysis, scripting, rehearsal and refinement – all parts of the process Smit outlines here.

Finally, and very importantly, the book is filled with encouraging illustrations of how his approach to "making values real" has led to personal as well as organisational break-throughs. Through these examples, readers can begin to apply the same insights to their own lives and experiences of values challenge.

Reading *Making Values Real* offers actionable guidance for anyone who wants to build values-driven leadership in themselves and in the organisations they work with or in. And for me, Arnold goes a long way to help resolve my own "crisis of faith." For that, and for his ongoing and impactful work, I am forever grateful.

PREFACE

Life is simultaneously a personal and relational journey. Inasmuch as we are unique in our individual existence, we are connected to others by the bonds of family, community, organisation, society and even the environment. In this interconnectedness, values play an important role in determining what we decide and to, how we relate and collaborate, and how we lead and follow. This, however, is easier said than done.

While values are ever-present and integrated into our very existence, we may struggle to consistently make them real. We often stumble in our boldest aspirations of integrating values into all aspects of our lives. While we value values such as honesty, respect, responsibility, fairness and compassion, we also have experience of their opposites and the challenges of upholding them under all circumstances. When we get values right, we harvest positive outcomes in personal, relational and organisational and societal terms. When values are violated, we suffer personal discomfort, relational damage, or even ethical failures with lasting consequences. It seems that even knowing the difference in outcomes between values valued and values violated does not guarantee that we will always succeed in making them real.

The challenge of making values real plays out in so many situations in life. It is present – often unconsciously so – in our decisions, actions, relationships, and attitudes. Some of our values-based experiences might be very personal and private, while others will inevitably be interpersonal and public. When we enjoy the positive and inspirational presence of values between ourselves and others, activities like communicating, collaborating and decision making mostly feel unproblematic. When values alignment breaks down and confrontation becomes inevitable – even imperative – the voicing of values might become very uncomfortable and speaking up a daunting challenge for many.

What does it take to make values real? What does it take to do this at home, in the neighbourhood, at work, and in society at large? How can this be the case in our close relationships, in our daily interactions and transactions, in our teams and boardrooms at work, in our stakeholder relationships in business and government, and among all citizens in society? What do we need to know and what skills do we need to master to enjoy the upside of a values-based life and minimise the outfalls of values neglect, compromise, and violation? These questions are at the heart of this book.

Without avoiding matters of definition and conceptual clarity, this book is not a theoretical quest but a guidebook for people who want to strengthen their ability to make values real in how they live, relate, work and lead. Having been involved in values work in teaching, training and organisational integration for almost a decade, I constantly encounter the challenges and questions of people who really want to live their values but often experience themselves as not being knowledgeable, skilful, or confident enough to do so in situations of moral discomfort, whether in their personal relationships, at work or in public. In these interactions, I have been privileged to observe the empowerment that people gain by mastering values conversations, working through values conflicts, building their capacity for personal moral agency and chancing their living and working environments. Personally, I have been so much enriched through these encounters – and stretched in my own understanding of values in concept and practice – that I cannot but write about it and share the learning value thereof more widely.

I write this book from the perspective of what I love doing most, namely, to facilitate transformative learning processes. A big part of the challenge of making values real is to go beyond naming and displaying them. It also goes beyond writing them up in codes and policies and demanding adherence under all circumstances. Beyond naming, values need to be explored for what they mean and why they matter in practice. Beyond stipulating preferred behaviours, values need to be mastered and embedded in situations of speech and argument covering the spectrum of ordinary conversations, stakeholder interactions and transactions, and boardroom deliberations and decisions. The lived experience of most people that I encounter in values work is that making values real is easier said than done. In the organisations they work for, they more often experience a gap between values espoused and values in practice. Hence, the leading question of this book is 'How can we make values real?'.

The book's title suggests that making values real is, metaphorically speaking, akin to the role that yeast plays in the baking of bread. Baking is both knowledge and art. The knowledge part is about ingredients and chemistry. The art part is about process, skills, taste and flavours. Bringing both together, the baker selects the ingredients, prepares the yeast, does the mixing and controls the conditions for the baking. The ultimate reward for this labour happens when the bread becomes a source of sustenance and the centre point of hospitality and community. However, nothing of this enjoyable outcome would be possible without the one essential ingredient, the yeast.

Values made real, represents in this book the yeast that we need for fulfilling relationships, meaningful work and decisions and actions that advance the ethical best that we are capable of. This realisation makes "bakers" of all of us. Like the baker, we live and work for value creation to put the proverbial bread on the table. Like the baker, we cannot afford to separate the economic benefits we are seeking from the ethical quality of what we are doing. Like the baker, we have to keep value creation in economic terms and values integration in ethical and relational terms closely related. By working like yeast, values are capable of mediating between these two processes, but only if we, the bakers, add them to the mix. There is for us much joy in getting this right and much pain in getting it wrong. Further in the book, we'll attend to both sides of the story.

It is my ideal that you, as the reader, experience this book as a guide for making values real in various situations. Like becoming adept at bread baking, we experience how values are learned, shaped, applied and challenged at home, at work and in public spheres. The book is intended to have relevance for all these situations, while, admittedly, there will be significantly more weight given to organisational perspectives. The latter is largely due to the fact that much of what I will be writing about has been stimulated by my work in organisational settings.

The book runs over eight chapters. The focus of chapter 1 will be on values as a concept in distinction from, but also related to ethics, virtues and rules. Chapter 2 is about the presence of values in our daily lives and how they function in our relationships, whether personal or at work. In chapter 3, we deal with values conflicts, what they are, how they come about and the rationalisations that often stand in the way of resolving them. In chapter 4, we deal with the question whether values conflicts can be resolved and how it can be done.

From the fifth chapter onwards, our focus shifts towards developing values-driven capacity in personal and organisational terms. In chapter 5, we deal with the potential of every values-conscious person to develop the confidence and competence for moral agency in their areas of influence and responsibility. Chapter 6 takes our quest to the seemingly evasive ideal of making values real in organisations. In chapter 7, we attend to the design and facilitation of values workshops. Chapter 8 concludes the book by pulling all the relevant insights into an integrated framework. Lastly, there is an appendix on page 143, referred to as a values playbook, which contains all the exercises referred to in the book combined with guidelines for using them in values-related activities.

There are several stories included in the book. Some of them straddle across chapters. They all stem from real-life situations. They mediate between theory and practice and connect the worlds of their actors with our own. Where necessary, care has been taken to obtain permission and anonymise the main characters and their organisations involved. I am immensely grateful for the privilege of using these narratives for the benefit of the book's readership.

This book is written at a time when there seems to be a hunger for making values real in the world. Due to multiple crises, we need to stand together and yet we are pulled or driven apart by competing ideologies and shallow solutions. We experience the impact of climate change, we pity the plight of migrants, we abhor the cruel impact of war on ordinary citizens, and we have come to distrust those in power whose only priority seems to be their own interests. My hope is that a rediscovery of the practical value of values will help us to embrace our common humanity, nourish our relationships, and help us work through our problems. We need more "bakers" in more places, working the yeast of values into the conversations, decisions, strategies and actions that may keep the dream of a better world alive.

In view of the above, I do not pretend that values hold the answers to all our grand challenges. What I do suggest is that making values real is a process that all values-minded people can participate in to make a difference in their areas of influence and responsibility. If you read the book as a leader who wants to instil a values-driven culture in your team, organisation or business, you may discover in it concepts, processes and practices that you can use for personal and organisational benefit. You may read it as a person in professional practice and discover applications for use in client-facing and other stakeholder encounters. If you read it as a human resource or organisational development practitioner, you may derive ideas of how values can be integrated into several organisational processes. In the case of being an ethics or compliance officer, you may find several helpful ideas to strengthen the effectiveness of your organisational mandate. Reading the book from the perspective of an employee in an organisation or a member of the public, mastering the ideas promoted in this book may empower you to act on your values more consistently over a broad range of situations. Although not academically inclined, the book may also be a helpful resource if you are a lecturer wanting to instil a values-driven learning environment or include teaching about values in your curricula. The point is not that the book is a one-size-fits-all creation. The point is that values are integral to who we are and how we are with others and that we are capable of developing the consciousness, confidence and competence to make values work in our daily existence.

March 2025

ACKNOWLEDGEMENTS

There are several people on my journey with values whom I am most grateful for. Standing out among them is Mary Gentile, globally renowned for her Giving Voice to Values approach. Her work informed much of my thinking on the connection between values and ethics. Reference to Mary's work will be present in many parts of the book. I owe her much gratitude and appreciate her willingness to write the foreword to the book.

In 2015, Mollie Painter-Morland, professor at Nottingham-Trent Business School, invited me to take part in the development of a values-driven leadership programme, initiated by the Brussels-based Academy of Business in Society. Participating in that project started my journey with values integration in educational and organisational environments. After initially co-facilitating programmes with Mollie, my circle of collaboration grew with Zilla North, Louis Jenkins, Elmé Viviers, and Bryan Robinson. I am immensely thankful for what we all could develop, present and/or write together.

Several other people contributed over the years to my understanding of the relationship between values, ethics, leadership, and organisational processes. While I can mention many more, I want to single out Deon Rossouw, Minka Woermann, Mias de Klerk, Barbara Pool, and Daniel Malan. I also owe thanks to Leon van Vuuren, who helped me with shaping the leading question of the book and Nico Simpson, who contributed greatly to the course material I use in values workshops.

Much of my understanding of what it takes to make values real was shaped by and in organisations. Some I have worked for and some I have worked with. In this regard, my gratitude includes Stellenbosch University, Stellenbosch Business School, The Ethics Institute, the Business Ethics Network of Africa, the Globally Responsible Leadership Initiative, Globethics.net, the Western Cape Department of Health's Eden District, Aalto University Executive Education, and the Uongozi Institute in Dar es Salaam. In February 2023, a student group of the Uongozi Institute gifted me a pen and challenged me to write a book on values. How could I say no?

My deepest gratitude is for Reinette, who encouraged me throughout this process and patiently endured my preoccupation with getting the book written.

Last but not least, I appreciate Knowledge Resources for taking this project on board and Cia Joubert for seeing it through to the end product it has become.

ABOUT THE AUTHOR

Arnold Smit is an extraordinary associate professor at Stellenbosch Business School and an associate professor in Management and Leadership at the IEDC-Bled School of Management in Slovenia. He is also the owner of WisePraxis (Pty) Ltd. His main interest is in the intersection of leadership, values and ethics, sustainability, and governance in organisations. Apart from teaching on these subjects in academic and corporate education programmes, he also facilitates organisational values workshops and integration processes. His conference presentations and publications include works on responsible leadership, values integration, corporate sustainability and responsibility, and multi-stakeholder process facilitation. In addition to other qualifications, he holds an Honours in Philosophy, a MPhil in Applied Ethics, and a Doctorate in Theology from Stellenbosch University. His career experience includes parish ministry, human resources management, management consulting, and management education. He also serves as a non-executive director of The Ethics Institute, a trustee of SEED Educational Trust, a member of the Globethics Pool of Experts, and as a fellow of the School for Social Innovation at Hugenote College.

CHAPTER 1

WHAT VALUES ARE ABOUT

> Values are core conceptions of the desirable within every individual and society.
>
> *Milton Rokeach*

INTRODUCTION

Having completed the admission of learners for the new year, the principal of a secondary school was approached by a parent requesting the late acceptance of his daughter. Upon declining the request, the parent answered with an exceptionally lucrative financial offer in exchange for his daughter's placement. Such money could go very far in boosting the future well-being and performance of the school. The parent persisted and so did the principal, three times in a row. Eventually, the parent had to back down and leave, with his daughter and all. Learning about this incident, I discussed it with the principal. She was very clear about her motivations. Prising her own *values*, and that of her school, trumped the *value* of the price money on the table. Her loyalty could not be bought, her integrity was not for sale, and she would never compromise fairness toward other learners and their families in her school's feeding area.

Why do values matter? For me? For you? For our organisations? For the world in which we happen to live? The short answer will be that values matter because they influence our attitudes, decisions, behaviours and actions across multiple situations, whether consciously or inadvertently.

We'd rather mostly be in situations where values flourish and infuse the ways in which we live, relate, work and lead. This is so much more productive than suffering the downside of values disagreement, challenge, and confrontation.

Values are real, whether invoked or not. There is rarely a situation in which values are not at the heart of what we think, say, decide or do. When these experiences echo our values, we hardly think about this connection consciously. When the opposite occurs, we might use value-specific terms to express our discomfort. Obviously, we'd like to have more of the former and less of the latter.

An important part of staying on the upside of making values real is to understand what values mean and why they are significant. This first chapter is, therefore, about conceptual housekeeping, the purpose of which is to develop a working understanding of values that we can use throughout the book. Apart from exploring the meaning of values from different viewpoints, we'll also discuss how values relate to ethics, virtues, and rules. The chapter concludes with some important propositions about values that will guide us throughout the book.

Values and value

To begin with, it is important to distinguish between something that we value and the values that we hold as commonly shared beliefs about human behaviours. In everyday language, we might notice the concept 'value' being used in a variety of ways. We often use 'value' in relation to productive and operational activities with measurable outcomes. We then refer to value creation and speak, for example, of shareholder or stakeholder value. We also use 'value' in referring to things that we appreciate and prefer for their benefit and usefulness, for example, income, job security, quality, comfort and safety. Similar to the former, we might hear people speak about how they value relational bonds and experiences which are dear to them, such as family, friendship, and collegiality. When looking at organisational values, we'll notice strategic and operational concepts such as excellence, innovation, teamwork and service, all premised on behaviours believed to enhance success and reputation.

In distinction from these things that we *value*, there are *values* which we hold for their intrinsic worth. With these values, we evaluate situations in which we need to distinguish between right and wrong and make decisions about appropriate behaviours and actions. These are ethical values and refer, for example, to concepts such as honesty, respect, responsibility, fairness, and compassion. These values are different from, but also at the same time critically related to the things that we value for their usefulness and benefit and the relationships and experiences we deem of special importance. For example, we value financial success but also want assurance that it was achieved in a manner that was honest, responsible and fair to all concerned. We may be quick to profess the importance of stakeholders for overall business success, but what values do they experience in how we treat them? The value that we place on personal comfort will be broadly granted, but when we pursue that to the expense of others, our values may become a point of contention. We may, therefore, say that there are multiple things that we *value* for the benefits that we may derive from them in distinction of the *values* that we hold for their intrinsic worth.

Some literature on values may help us to further expand our understanding of the different ways in which values are defined, categorised, and applied. Rokeach[1] refers to values as "core conceptions of the desirable within every individual and society" and highlights the role they play, for example, in guiding our actions, judgements, choices, attitudes, evaluations, arguments, rationalisations, and explanations for certain outcomes. Rokeach[2] further makes the interesting distinction between "terminal or ends values" as beliefs about desirable states of existence worth striving for (for example, happiness or wisdom) and "instrumental or means values" as beliefs about desirable modes of behaviour (for example, honesty and responsibility). The relation between the two types seems to be that the latter is instrumental in the ethical attainment of the former.

According to Gentile[3] the word 'values' suggests "something that we own ourselves and hold dear" and the "inherent worth and quality of a thing or idea". It is especially the moral or ethical dimension of values that attracts her attention. She points, furthermore, to a process of convergence across millennia and cultures that led to a widely shared list of core values that most people will agree with, namely, honesty, respect, responsibility, fairness, and compassion. This collective of values is central to the Giving Voice to Values (GVV) method that she has become globally renowned for and that we will frequently revisit throughout this book.

Freeman and Auster[4] focus on the role of values in organisations and go in a somewhat different direction than Gentile with her more individualised approach. While acknowledging that understanding values as "preferences expressed in our behaviours" makes the study thereof easier, they also want to guard against the assumption that our values are stable and that we always know what they are. Instead of focusing on a core list, like Gentile does, they argue in favour of values that might change in relation to how we grow and develop and how our personal and shared narratives evolve over time. Emphasising the relational and contextual nature of values they prefer to think of values emerging from and creating meaning in the conversations that we have with other people. Values can be of a personal, organisational and societal nature, and in these layers, values might overlap or conflict. They therefore prefer a conversational approach towards identifying and shaping values and propose the application of four complementary perspectives, namely, introspection (how we reflect on the world around us), connectedness (how we relate and collaborate), history (the influence of our past) and aspiration (our hopes and dreams in relation to the greater good).

In between Gentile's focus on a core set of commonly shared values and Freeman and Auster's preference for the dynamic emergence of values, we find others who highlight different kinds of values. Rossouw and Van Vuuren[5] regard values "as relatively stable convictions about what is important but not to be equated with ethics". With their core interest in business ethics and organisations they distinguish strategic values (reflected in vision and mission statements) and work values (the priorities that employees should adhere to in their jobs) from ethical values (that which relates to the relations and interactions between stakeholders). Groenewald and Dondé[6] distinguish between societal (shared by members of a community), professional (determined by a professional body), corporate/organisational (what an organisation expects its employees to apply - strategic, work and ethical) and personal (principles and beliefs of individuals, guidance in decision making) values.

Speaking of societal values, we may also look at a few foundational documents in which the importance of values is emphasised. The Universal Declaration of Human Rights[7] contains values-related concepts such as dignity, equality, freedom, justice and peace. The Constitution of South Africa, and more specifically the Bill of Rights[8] contained in it, emphasises the notions of human equality, dignity and freedom. The King IV Report on Corporate Governance for South Africa[9] prioritises the values of integrity, competence, responsibility, accountability, fairness, and transparency for the governance duties of boards and directors. These, and several similar documents, make a very clear point: values matter, for and among individuals and within organisations and societies.

In summary, we might say that values refer to deeply held beliefs that guide our attitudes, behaviours and judgements, as individuals, but also in our relationships, organisations and societies.

As a working definition, we may regard values as the aspirational beliefs that we hold about human behaviours expressing how we prefer or agree to live and relate and determining what we regard as right or wrong in particular situations and the decisions we make as a result.

Values and ethics

There can hardly be a conversation about values without reference to ethics. The question often is, which of the two to deal with first? We have good reason to say that our values inform our ethics. At the same time, there is also an argument to be made for ethics as the umbrella without which our conversations about values can hardly be meaningful.

Two related Greek words, ethos and ethikos, offer us a good starting point for the discussion. According to the Merriam-Webster Dictionary[10] 'ethos' refers to "the distinguishing character, sentiment, moral nature, or guiding beliefs of a person, group, or institution". Stemming from the same root, 'ethic' (singular) may refer to "a theory or system of moral values", "the principles of conduct governing an individual or a group", a "consciousness of moral importance", or "a guiding philosophy". In the plural, 'ethics' means "a set of moral issues or aspects" or "the discipline dealing with what is good and bad and with moral duty and obligation". The interplay between 'ethos' (character, nature and beliefs) on the one hand and 'ethics' (theory, principles and philosophy) on the other is noteworthy. Making values real involves the translation of ethos into ethics, character into conduct, and beliefs into action as we navigate through the moral challenges that we are confronted with in lived reality.

Since the early conceptualisations of ethics among the ancient Greeks about 2500 years ago, the field has evolved into different ethical theories and areas of application. The three most common theories refer to duties (to do what is right or based on rights), consequences (achieving a good state of affairs or the greatest good for the greatest number of people) and virtues (referring to the goodness of character). Each of these theories enjoys strong support, opens valuable pathways for working through ethical challenges and faces fierce criticism for their shortcomings. While an ethics of duty highlights the importance of rights, it also raises concerns about the sources of normativity that its proponents may build their arguments on. Exercising ethical reasoning from the perspective of consequences might stimulate realism and foresight about outcomes, but the ever-present risk is that the end will justify the means, notwithstanding the harm that may result. When considering character, we would like to count on good people consistently doing good things, but we must remain alert to human fallibility in the face of temptation and the risks associated with hubris and bad judgement.

As the philosophical scope of ethics theories expanded over time, so did theories of applied ethics as well. Among the most prominent areas of applied ethics today, and for very good reasons too, we will find bioethics, environmental ethics, techno-ethics, and business ethics. The latter is of specific relevance for this book, especially in view of its prominent connection to values integration in organisations. Crane and Matten[11] argue that business ethics is occupied with the values that drive business decisions. From a normative perspective, it comes down to the distinction between what is right and wrong for an individual or community (as determined by norms, values and beliefs) and the rules and principles by which that is defined (for example, duty, consequences or virtue). From a descriptive perspective, ethical decision making is about understanding the individual and/or situational factors that have an influence on whether people make morally right or wrong decisions. This distinction does not only tap into the ethos - ethics relationship referred to earlier, but calls for consideration of contextual influences as well.

Also focusing on business ethics, Rossouw and Van Vuuren[12] bring a relational and action-orientated angle to the definition of ethics, stating that it "concerns itself with what is right and good in human interaction" and revolves around the concepts of the self, the good and the other. Translating this to business ethics, they state that it "is about a conception of what is good (values and standards) that guide the business (self) in its interaction with others (stakeholders)". The 'good' thus needs to be given substance in order to determine the quality of such an interaction and make it evaluable in terms of being either right or wrong. Values play an indispensable role in this process.

In summary, values and ethics are different but closely related. While values are deeply held beliefs and principles that guide our attitudes, behaviours and judgements, ethics provide a values-based framework for navigating complex situations and interactions. While values shape ethics by providing the criteria for the evaluation of actions and decisions, ethics express values by translating them into actionable decisions and behaviours. While this sounds straightforward and easy, getting it right does not come without challenges.

Values and virtues

The conceptual relationship between values and virtues is an important one to clarify. It so often happens that we confuse the two, especially because of the semantic overlaps that we find between them. While values are about beliefs and principles that guide attitudes, behaviours and judgement, virtues refer to qualities and traits that individuals cultivate within themselves.

We can hardly discuss virtues without going back to Aristotle's understanding thereof. Mintz[13] explains how the Greeks were less interested in actions that were universally morally right and more in the best sort of life that human beings can live. The ultimate purpose of life, in the Greek tradition, was to attain a life of excellence. The Greek word for excellence is 'arete', the translation of which is 'virtue'. While both Socrates and Plato contributed their part in explaining what a life of excellence is about, Aristotle eventually became the most prominent voice in this conversation. Aristotle, as Mintz explains, spoke of two types of virtue, namely intellectual ones, such as wisdom and understanding, and moral ones, such as generosity and self-control. The first can be taught; the latter is formed by habit. Combined, they enable us to exercise practical wisdom and take proper action. While Aristotle mentions several virtues, four are often ascribed to his take on a life of excellence, namely prudence, temperance, courage and justice. These are also referred to as the so-called 'cardinal virtues'.

It is significant to note how virtues eventually became part of the Positive Organisational Scholarship movement in the early 2000s. Picking up from the Aristotelian tradition, Park and Peterson[14] write about the importance of virtues for both individuals and organisations. Connecting virtues with character strengths, they discuss six core virtues that encapsulates our understanding of human goodness, namely, wisdom and knowledge, courage, love, justice, temperance, and transcendence.

Much more can be said about virtues, but for our purposes it suffices to note that virtues and values are connected. The enactment of values is inspired by the expression of virtues as character strengths. To enact values, on the other hand, confirms and strengthens the development of character and virtues.

Values and rules

For conceptual housekeeping, we also need to explore one more relationship, namely that between values and rules. We understand values by now as beliefs that guide our attitudes, decisions and behaviours. Rules, on the other hand, are specific directives or regulations that dictate what is allowed or prohibited in different contexts. Rules are made to ensure order and consistency and demand compliance in a given situation. Not following the rules, will normally be met by some form of sanction or penalty. Without indulging in extensive analysis, we can point to different kinds of rules, for example, the laws of a country, the policies of an organisation, technical and procedural prescriptions, codes of conduct in professions, and, last but not least, the rules for games and sports.

We can therefore say that values are principle-based while rules are command-based; that values apply across various aspects of life, while rules are more situation-specific; and that values come from within, while rules are externally imposed. Schoeman[15] summarises it aptly when saying that "rules aim primarily to achieve compliance, while values aim primarily for commitment.

Notwithstanding the different nature and objectives of values and rules, it should be the ideal that values and rules reciprocally enable the expression of each other. This being said, values may also stand in a critical relationship to rules when they are deemed to be unfair, or not consistently or fairly applied.

Why does conceptual clarity matter?

We are pursuing the question of how we can make values real across various spheres of life: individually, in our relationships, at work, and in society. Understanding values and their relatedness to ethics, virtues and rules seems to be an important part of our quest. Following from the preceding sections, our argument is that *virtues* are about the kind of people we aspire to be and be known for, that *values* are about the ways in which we express these character traits through our attitudes, decisions and behaviours in interactional situations, that *rules* provide us with conduct prescriptions in specific situations and that *ethics* provides us with the means to analyse, evaluate and plan for action according to moral standards of right and wrong in relation to specific situations.

We assume that people with character strengths such as prudence, temperance, courage and justice, to name but these few, will desire to act according to personal and interpersonal values such as honesty, respect, responsibility, fairness and compassion in the interactions and transactions they engage with in different situations and thereby strengthen the ethos and ethics of the relationships, organisations, communities and societies they partake in. At the same time, we realise that situations can become murky and that this complementarity that we seek between virtues, values, rules and ethics can become daunting and may even fall apart. Making values real is both aspirational and imperative; getting it done requires wisdom and courage.

Let's take the Covid-19 pandemic as an example. The pandemic, still fresh in our memories, was a living laboratory of what it means to make values real. It literally connected the practice of values with the preservation of life and relationships. While science was driving the search for knowledge and treatment and public governance and policy laid down the rules for behaviours, we as the general public, had to make decisions about our daily activities and interpersonal conduct. We soon discovered that rules could at best provide us with a baseline set of behavioural prescriptions and prohibitions, while the largest proportion of decisions were left to us to make in view of our values. We were called upon to think carefully about the information we relied on and share, to be transparent about our own state of health and be truthful about our whereabouts in potentially risky contact with others. We were called upon to treat everyone else – irrespective of their standing or influence – with dignity, to make their health and safety a priority as if our own and to honour their personal space through social distancing. We had to think carefully about what we decide and do, especially in view of the consequences that it may have had for others. While we needed to care for and protect ourselves, we had to consider the rightful interests of others, too. Before stocking up as much as we could, we had to think about our needs for household supplies and medicines in relation to that of fellow citizens and healthcare facilities. While income streams dropped, businesses had to carefully consider their layoff approach. And, to top it all, there was the difficult tension to manage between the demand for social distancing in relation to caring for loved ones needing our presence and comfort. All of the above were intermingled with tense debates about the existence of the virus and the trustworthiness of the vaccines on the one hand and people who behaved as if there were no pandemic on the other. Covid-19 was indeed a laboratory of what it means to make values real.

Core propositions

In the preface, I mentioned that I write this book from a facilitator's perspective. My goal is not to indulge in scholarly discourse and resolve all the debatable issues around values. Focusing on process, I want the book to be an empowering resource for making values real and actionable in how we live, relate, work, and lead. I, therefore, propose four core propositions that I regard as essential guidelines in the journey with values ahead of us.

Values are life-giving

Values have an aspirational and inspirational quality. They present an invitation to be our best individual and collective selves as we interact, make decisions, and engage together in the pursuit of common goals and ideals. Making values real infuses our relationships, organisations, communities and societies with life-giving positive qualities. We should therefore guard against invoking or talking about values only when there is trouble at stake.

Values flourish in relationships

We experience the presence and potential of values in relationships. It is among others that values become real for us and enable us to reap the benefits of their enactment in our relationally embedded human existence. While values make meaningful relationships possible, they also inspire us to collaborate well and achieve great things together. Therefore, inasmuch as values are personally held beliefs, their realisation holds great potential for our relationships and interactions at home, at work, and in society at large.

Values endure human vulnerability

While values are aspirational expressions of the best we can be, we also know that we are not always our best selves and that our relationships suffer detrimental consequences when values are neglected, compromised, or violated. It might not be an overstatement to argue that all of us can tell stories of having let ourselves and others down, or being let down by others, as a result of not being consistent in how we make values real.

Our values do not cease to exist in these troublesome situations but offer us pathways for building back, however difficult it may be. I often mention in workshops that values are not about human perfection; they are about meaningful co-existence.

Values are nurtured through conversations

Values statements abound in organisations and so too the pessimism about their meaning and usefulness. The mere fact that they appear next to mission and vision statements doesn't guarantee that they are understood and mastered in practice. For values to come to life and influence attitudes, decisions and behaviours to the extent they are meant to do, requires ongoing conversations and consistent application. Values are rarely a concern where our relationships flourish and we are aligned with what is good and right in our decisions and actions. It is when something is morally questionable that we are tested for our adherence to our personal and shared values and challenged to have conversations that help us to stay ethical.

Conclusion

We are pursuing the question of how we can make values real. This chapter offered us a first step towards an answer, namely, that we need to understand what values are about, and why they are important for how we live, relate, work and lead. Defining values in distinction of, but also in relation to ethics, virtues and rules, is important for conceptual clarity. Hence our working definition of values as the aspirational beliefs that we hold about human behaviours expressing how we prefer or agree to live and relate and determining what we regard as right or wrong in particular situations and the decisions we make as a result.

With our working definition in mind, we affirm the importance of values in personal, relational, organisational, and societal terms. Values, when upheld, work like yeast by enabling virtuousness and ethicality across all these spheres. When values are violated, we are faced with the challenging task of building back. Hereafter, we'll be exploring the meaning of five core values in daily life and how we might benefit or lose by either upholding or compromising them.

There is a reflective exercise at the end of each chapter in the book. These exercises are for thoughtful engagement with how we can make values real. Each exercise will take you one step further on your journey with values.

Regular reflection can be a very empowering practice for making values real. While we will pay specific attention to mastering reflection in chapter 5, I encourage you to combine it with the reading of the book from the very beginning. If you are already used to a practice of regular reflection, you may take the opportunity to make the reading of this book part of it. Add to your journal those insights that you find useful while you read and go deeper with the reflective exercise at the end of each chapter. If written reflection is new for you, think about opening a journal and use the exercise at the end of each chapter as a starting point. You may just be surprised by what you are discovering about yourself and the role that values play in your life.

So, let's make a start. Think about yourself in the context of your relationships and responsibilities. Specifically, think about the various kinds of interactions that you have with others and then reflect on the following questions:

- What values guide your attitudes, decisions and actions in these situations?
- Where did you get these values come from and why do they matter to you?
- What do you do to make your values real?
- What challenges do you experience in making your values real?

Hold on to your reflections on these questions as we will open another window on them at the end of chapter 2.

CHAPTER 2

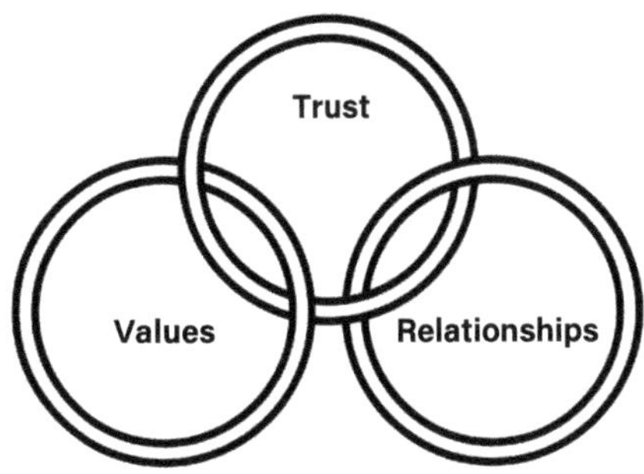

WHY VALUES MATTER

> Getting the words right, does not mean getting the values right.
>
> —*Freeman and Auster*

INTRODUCTION

Presenting at a conference of The Ethics Institute several years ago, the board chair of a South African retail group shared with the audience the dismissal of a director who was caught with unpaid shaving blades in his pocket. The incident happened at one of the group's outlets. The said person was searched and reported by a security guard controlling the exit to the staff's parking facility. The director's explanation was that he paid an inspection visit to the shop floor and, upon passing the relevant shelf, he realised he needed shaving blades. His excuse was that when he left, he simply forgot to pay. The chair was unwavering in his judgement. His explanation was threefold. Firstly, he expects the highest standard of conduct from directors. Secondly, the security guard should be praised for having exercised his duties so diligently. And, thirdly, not long before the director's misstep, they dismissed a cashier at the same shop for stealing school stationery for her child. What counts for the gander, counts for the goose. Essentially, it is about fairness and equality.

Whenever I use this vignette in workshops, the reaction of participants ranges across three positions. There are those who agree with immediate dismissal, those who propose suspension followed by a proper investigation, and those who accept the director's excuse combined with a warning to be more cautious in the future. Whatever the preferred approach, values and how they are understood and applied are written large over the discussions.

We are no strangers to values. They are real and present wherever we interact with the world around us. Values are part of our thoughts and language. Especially in situations in which we feel challenged, leading us to think or say that something is against our values. Even more so are we surrounded by the values statements of organisational brands vying for attention, trying to convince us of their good intentions, reputations, and the benefits of their products or services. Most organisations will almost certainly have a statement of values supposed to guide people's behaviour in matters of strategic, operational, relational and ethical performance. And yet, despite all these stated values, it does not mean that they are understood, embraced and consistently applied. It is like Freeman and Auster[16] saying, "getting the words right, doesn't mean getting the values right".

The challenge, for many people, is in going beyond naming values towards understanding what they mean in practice and mastering the processes of making them real and doing so confidently and consistently.

So, we seem to have a challenge. We have no shortage of values concepts, whether holding them personally or being introduced to the values of other people or organisations. The challenge is not in the naming of the values, having them on the walls, displaying them on marketing collateral, having them enshrined in codes and creeds, or drumming them up in public statements.

In the preface, I referred to writing this book from a facilitator's perspective. In the discussion that follows, I focus on three things. Firstly, I introduce a process for exploring the meaning of values. Secondly, I demonstrate the usefulness of this approach by applying it to a set of five commonly accepted values. Lastly, I will discuss some of the challenges we encounter in making values real, especially in situations when more than one value competes for our attention at the same time.

Throughout the chapter, my focus will be on reporting the lived experience of participants as observed and recorded in the values conversations and workshops that I facilitated in over several years.

Making sense of values

In values workshops, I usually focus on four themes: the meaning and significance of values, what values conflicts are about, how values conflicts might be resolved, and the integration of values in relationships, teamwork, leadership and other organisation-specific activities. In this chapter, our focus will be on the meaning and significance of values. The other themes will be attended to in later chapters.

It is not uncommon for us to name our values. Neither is it strange for us to be working in organisations where several values are listed in statements, codes and policies. It is the translation of these values in practical terms and the common agreement of what they mean which is most often amiss. Conversations about meaning, practice and neglect or violation bring the values to life and make them useful in relation to situations in practice.

As discussed until now, values sets or statements appear in different forms, depending on the people or organisation involved. As a baseline and starting point for a values conversation, I work with three questions:

- What does this value mean for us in practice?
- What do we gain from practicing this value?
- What results from neglecting or violating this value?

Relating their values to these three questions has an empowering effect on conversation participants. While clarifying the meaning and use of their values in conversation, they also become used to using them in communication with others. I often find that people appreciate the value of values conversations exactly for improving their personal and collective understanding of what values mean and how they apply to their lived experiences in practice.

Five common values in practice

I have indicated in chapter 1 that I appreciate Mary Gentile's preference for five core globally accepted values, namely honesty, respect, responsibility, fairness and compassion.[17] The point is not that there are no other values to mention, neither does it negate the dynamic process of the emergence of new values or the shifts in values preferences over time, as advocated for by Freeman and Auster[18]. I make the choice in the interest of process and method. As this book unfolds, I will introduce you to ways of working through values clarification, resolving of values conflicts, integrating values into relationships, leadership, teamwork and organisational activities and functions. This core set of five values is sufficient to demonstrate the pathways that we can follow to enhance our efforts with making values real.

In the discussion that follows I will introduce a blend of workshop participants' insights and my personal observations to bring out the meaning and significance of the five chosen values under discussion. What follows illustrates that people know very well what these values mean, what we benefit from upholding them and what we lose from neglecting or violating them. Why we often land up in trouble with them is a conversation for the next chapter.

Honesty

We might call honesty the value that represents truthfulness and openness in our dealings with others. Other associations that usually come to mind include integrity and authenticity. From a virtues perspective, honesty is very much associated with the character of a person. However, from a values perspective we are interested in how honesty affects relationships. In connection with honesty, workshop participants highlight and appreciate behaviours such as telling the truth, the ability to speak openly, to be inclusive in communication, and to be able to have hard conversations when needed.

What do we gain from practicing honesty? Workshop participants consistently associate the presence of honesty with the trust it builds in people, information and processes. Secondly, honesty, benefits communication, making information believable as well as enabling critical and constructive feedback. Furthermore, the presence of honesty within a team benefits their sense of cohesion, collaboration, openness and productivity. And, lastly, honesty enhances stakeholder relations and reputation too.

People have no difficulty in identifying the consequences of honesty being violated. First of all, it undermines trust followed by a domino effect on relationships, teamwork, and communication. Distrust easily turns into suspicion, secretiveness, second guessing and micro-management. Once broken, the rebuilding of trust is not impossible, but it is a hard task. Broken trust, due to dishonesty, affect relationships across the spectrum from the most intimate (as in households) to the relatively formal (as in organisations, stakeholder relations and society at large).

In summary, where honesty is upheld, there is a high level of trust which, in turn, benefits communication, collaboration and productivity. Where honesty is compromised, trust is broken, and conversations become overshadowed by scepticism and suspicion. The impact of the latter on productivity in a team or organisation is self-evident.

Respect

Our understanding of respect starts with the dignity and regard that we experience in our interactions with one another. It reflects the way in which we value, recognise, acknowledge and appreciate our shared humanity. Respect shows up in perceptions, body language, tone of voice and how we listen and respond to others. Respect is considerate and unconditional and not premised on position, rank, gender, ethnicity, culture, religion, capabilities or sexual orientation.

We like to think that respect should presuppose reciprocity as something that is both given and earned. While there is much truth in this assumption, there is more to it. Respect is both a need and a gift. It is the need that each of us have for being valued for who we are, as well as the gift of dignity we grant to others, whether they acknowledge or deserve it or not. As one workshop participant so aptly said: "Respect is not so much earned or given as it is built".

If the above is what respect in action means, what will then be the upside of upholding it in relationships, for example, at work? Where there is respect, people feel accepted, valued, and appreciated. Such conditions translate into a happy work environment, characterised by synergy, collegiality, collaboration, support, teamwork and productivity. Where there is respect, people experience more freedom and confidence to exercise their skills and voice their opinions.

The neglect or violation of respect has dire consequences for relationships. Disrespect causes disengagement manifesting in people becoming withdrawn, minimising their contributions and becoming disinvested in the common cause of a relationship, a group or organisation. At a deeper personal level, disrespect causes hurt, shame, self-doubt, lack of confidence and even fear. One step further we enter the terrain of anger, resentment and conflict. The impact of disrespect on relationships manifests in the breakdown of communication, collaboration, performance and productivity. Eventually disrespect breeds disrespect - a vicious cycle indeed.

In addition to the above, I must add that respect is a subtle value that involves more than just how we speak to or treat others. We cannot talk of respect without reference to power, gender, and culture. It might well be that the association of respect with power, might lead to fear of speaking up against people in senior positions. It is also possible that in patriarchal cultures, women and youth are expected to "know their place" and refrain from confronting male elders. Furthermore, in intercultural interactions, much misunderstanding might result around practices of greeting, conversing and/or eating. Respect, we might say, is beyond given and earned, also learned.

Responsibility

Most people, it seems, associate responsibility with a job description, a role definition, and the execution of tasks according to prescribed rules and regulations and taking accountability for the results. What I constantly hear in values workshops is that upholding responsibility in personal terms, translates into good teamwork. Teams do better when everyone takes responsibility and contributes to getting a job done. Where everyone contributes and does their part, the job becomes easier for all, improving efficiency, performance and productivity. Working in such a synergistic environment also has an empowering impact on participants; they grow and develop as a result of the positive example and encouragement of one another.

Compromising responsibility has the opposite effect. Where responsibility falters, the job does not get done, standards might become compromised, and important targets or deadlines might be missed. Moreover, teamwork and team spirit get eroded where some members might not be pulling their part. Should any person in a team not fulfil their responsibilities or not being held accountable for such neglect, extra work must be taken up by others. The latter easily turns into complaints about uneven workloads and additional working hours combined with accusations of unfairness. Consequently, the potential for blame shifting, conflict and disengagement might increase. The spill over into stakeholder relations and reputational risk is self-evident.

While the above understanding of responsibility is an acceptable starting point, there is more to it. Responsibility also calls for proactive awareness and consideration in what we say, decide and do. If we accept the relational nature and embeddedness of values, as stated in chapter 1, it follows that what we say, decide or do will have consequences for the multiple relationships that we are partaking in. These relationships include those that are more personal, those that are work-related and those that are of general societal relevance. In all these circles of relatedness and influence, responsibility requires from us to partake as mindful and considerate human beings who seek the best interest and most sustainable outcomes for all concerned. Responsibility, however important it might be in the context of work, is also a proactive and responsive orientation to life. It is the expression of a unique human capability to respond meaningfully and appropriately to the demands and challenges of being human, in individual and collective terms. It also expresses what it means to care for and live in harmony with the societal and environmental systems that we are dependent upon for our sustenance and continued and sustainable existence. The responsible person, so understood, will therefore also be a mindful participant in relationships, in meetings, and operational settings, to ensure that decisions, behaviours and actions are not just aimed at internally focused and short-term gains, but above else also take long-term consequences into account.

Fairness

Naturally, and almost inadvertently, people equate fairness with equality in treatment and opportunity. Circling further out, workshop participants will refer to the fair allocation of resources, the balancing of workloads and the consistent application of policies and procedures. One step further and equity becomes added to the conversation and shifts the focus to matters of history, context, redress and diversity. Equality and equity add breadth to our understanding of fairness. Equality refers to having access to the same resources and opportunities. Equity takes individual contexts, differences and needs into account to achieve fair outcomes regarding access to resources and opportunities. There is an inherent complexity in this conversation, especially in South Africa where you can hardly separate any conversation about fairness from equality and equity.

Upholding fairness makes everyone feel worthy. Where fairness dominates, people feel valued, included and supported. Teamwork benefits when people feel they belong, are appreciated for what they contribute and are developed and empowered according to their needs and interests. In this way, fairness contributes to a flourishing workplace with improved collaboration and satisfaction for all concerned. It needs to be added, though, that fairness in combination with the embrace of equity and diversity, requires a learning process which, if maintained, bodes well for long-term success in organisations.

What if fairness is violated? From an emotional perspective, one can expect feelings of discontent, distrust and resentment. Behaviourally, unfairness may suppress motivation, engagement and productivity. Teamwork may suffer while conflict might increase. Procedurally, people might argue that rights have been violated, that discrimination is perpetuated, and that bias has overruled justice.

I want to add two reflections on this discussion. I often ask people, who are parents, about the first values-related word they hear their small children speak. It is not long before someone will say "this is unfair!", tantrums included. Why is this the case? Why do we have from such a young age a perception about what fairness is, whether justified or not?

I think it is because fairness is the one value that speaks to comparison between people. It is for us, whether young or old, a very sensitive issue, namely, to be fairly treated, and to experience equality in comparison to others. And beyond fairness and equality, equity requires from us a deeper understanding of justice in practice and a learning curve to talk about how to make it work. My advice to people is to always remember that, once the horse of unfairness has bolted, it is very difficult to do reparations afterwards. Therefore, when it comes to procedural fairness in promotions, appointments and procurement processes, it is very important to clarify and agree beforehand on all criteria concerned and on how a transparent decision-making process might best be followed.

Compassion

We usually associate compassion with empathy, kindness, caring and love. Compassion invites us to be aware and considerate about the circumstances and well-being of others. Through a sense of shared humanity, we talk about "putting yourself in other people's shoes" by attending to their hardships and noticing their special circumstances. Compassion is, furthermore, expressed in how we get in touch, how we listen, how we understand, and how we create hospitality for fellow human beings. Should the same become bestowed on us, we feel seen and heard and experience recognition and inclusion. Through compassion, the golden rule of "doing unto others" becomes for us a lived reality.

Where compassion is upheld and practiced, people feel appreciated, heard, understood, loved, supported and cared for. In a working environment the expression of compassion translates into joy, engagement, loyalty and productivity. People might be willing to give back more, to make an effort of mutual support and to get to know the human being behind the job description. Through compassion we make gains in collegiality, unity, trust and open communication.

On the opposite side of compassion upheld there are several negative consequences. The neglect or violation of compassion manifests in feelings of alienation, isolation, loneliness, and unhappiness. The workplace might be experienced as cold, harsh and impersonal. Behaviours such as withdrawal or quiet quitting, inevitably impacts on teamwork, performance and productivity. Even worse, these adverse consequences might transfer to stakeholder relationships and cause negative perceptions and reputational damage. The lack of caring on the inside of an organisation may transfer to a lack of caring and indifference towards those on the outside.

Compassion seems like the easiest value to talk about. However, it also comes with its own challenges. Inasmuch as it is meant to be a gift to others, it can be abused, whether in personal or formal relationships. Furthermore, compassion might suffer accusations of favouritism if there is a suspicion that everyone does not get a fair share of it. With one of my client organisations, I have noticed how appreciative people were for the compassion shown by their employer during the Covid pandemic. More recently some of the same people were complaining about the post-pandemic differentiation in working arrangements and asked why some staff must now be office-bound while others may continue to work remotely. "How fair is that?" they now ask.

The interrelatedness of values

When we enter relational space, whether in conversations, meetings, decision-making processes or general public interactions, we enter domains in which values are already an embedded and present reality.

In closing this chapter, I want to share a few observations about the interrelatedness of values, both in terms of our relational existence and in terms of how the values are interconnected with one another. In chapter 1, I referred to values as being personally embodied and relationally embedded. While we must take personal ownership for the values that we care about and express them in attitude, word and deed in a variety of situations, we do not own them per se. There is a point to be made that they belong to humanity and that their meaning and variety of expressions have been shaped over centuries in households, communities and various institutions in societies. Yes, individually we own, embrace and express values, whether consciously or inadvertently, but in essence their existence transcends us. From the preceding conversation around five very common values, we realised how definitive, how real and practical, and how consequential values can be for how we live and relate and how we work and collaborate. When we uphold the values at stake, we gain and when we don't, we lose.

Because of the essential interrelatedness and relational embeddedness of values, none of them can be separated from the other. While we, for example, might experience a violation of honesty, it does have repercussions for respect and responsibility. Similarly, showing compassion towards one person cannot be disconnected from fairness to others. Should fairness, especially in procedural terms, be violated, accusations of dishonesty and lack of transparency will follow soon.

The preceding discussion about values should also be considered in relation to some of the debates referred to in chapter 1. The choice to focus on five common moral values for the purposes of this book, might come across as limited. However, given the process of communicative meaning-making that I propose in this and other chapters, we notice the capability of ordinary people to understand, discuss and integrate these values into their contextually determined relationships and working environments.

Making values real presupposes that there is work to be done. As individuals we have a stake in the benefits of a values-driven existence, but it requires from us awareness about our attitudes, behaviours and actions across a wide range of human interactions. In organisations, it represents a special challenge for managers and leaders to create values-driven working relationships and environments. Organisations succeeding in this, will reap the benefits; those who don't will reap undesirable outcomes. Somewhere Peter Drucker aptly phrased the challenge: "Only three things happen naturally in organisations: friction, confusion and underperformance. Everything else, requires leadership". I dare to add that upholding values are part of this task.

Conclusion

In this chapter, I argued for a process-based approach for exploring the meaning of values in the lived experiences of people across the varieties of situations and relationships they operate in.

We engaged more thoroughly with five globally accepted moral values through the understanding and experience of people working in organisations. We discovered the following about each of these values:

- Honesty is the value that demands truthfulness and transparency in our dealings with one another.
- Respect is the value that speaks to the dignity and regard that we experience in our interactions with one another.
- Responsibility is the value that calls for proactive awareness and consideration in what we say, decide and do.
- Fairness is the value that makes us sensitive for comparison in treatment and thereby sharpens our sense of justice.
- Compassion is the value that invites us to be aware and considerate of the circumstances and well-being of others.

Are values real? Yes, they are. Do we always succeed in making them real? No, we don't. We know it from experience. Values work like yeast in our relationships. Ensuring that the yeast works, bring us multiple benefits. Leaving the yeast out or simply adding it unprepared, leaves us disappointed.

Coming up, our focus will be on giving voice to values in situations of values conflict. More than understanding values and appreciating their wholesome presence in various situations, making values real is dependent on how we voice them under pressure and in the turmoil of values conflicts.

The questions at the end of chapter 1 prompted you to think about values that guide your decisions and actions in relationships and responsibilities. I am wondering how the discussion of the five common values in this chapter connects with the values that you have identified in that reflective exercise. What similarities or differences did you identify? How did this chapter further enrich your understanding of values?

Taking the next step, I invite you to identify at least two important relationships that you are involved in, for example, one more personal (family or friends) and the other more work-related (colleagues, team, customers, or suppliers). Considering the following questions, reflect on how values influence your experience of these relationships:

- Who are the people involved in each of these relationships?
- Which values stand out for you in your interactions with them?
- In these relationships, what benefits do you experience in upholding these values?
- In these relationships, have you experienced the neglect or violation of any values and what resulted from it?
- What can you do to strengthen the presence and practice of values in these relationships?

CHAPTER 3

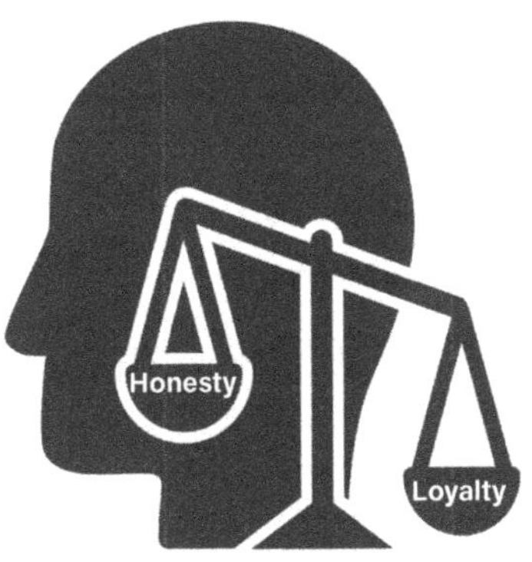

VALUES CONFRONTED

> An agent with a strong will and poor imagination does not fail to do what she knows she should, rather she feels that she should do *something*, but does not know what.
>
> —*Mavis Biss*

INTRODUCTION

During the time of the Covid-19 pandemic, and shortly after being promoted to be the clinical manager in a metro clinic, Agatha was confronted with a difficult situation. She noticed a senior district manager taking antibiotics without prescription. This being a senior person, confronted Agatha with a tough dilemma: "Do I confront or report her, or do I keep quiet?" Apart from expecting conflict, fear of victimisation was her biggest concern.

In this almost fleeting incident, we notice the power asymmetry between the two individuals. The junior one is, among other things, responsible for the stock and procedures under her control. The senior one, on the other hand, has control over the people under her command, the clinical manager included. The best time to do something about this situation is there and then, but Agatha seems overwhelmed by the potential consequences. It is not difficult to have sympathy with her.

Whether invoked or not, implicitly experienced or explicitly stated, our values reveal much of who we are, what we aspire to, how we evaluate situations in life, what we decide, how we act, and how we either associate with or differentiate ourselves from others.

Values, more than what we may realise, is not a subject for special occasions and conversations. Values are present in what we feel, think, say and decide about the variety of situations that we are daily confronted with. In some situations, such as conversations, meetings, decisions, actions, we might be personally involved. Other situations, we might experience or observe more indirectly and have positive or negative thoughts and feelings about. Interestingly, when in situations in which we experience values congruence, we may seldom hear it being explicitly referred to. However, when there is discord between what we believe our values to be and that which we experience or observe, it raises the need for making values explicit.

There are, therefore, two sides to making values real. First and foremost, we would like to experience more of the benefits of values confirmed and less of the consequences of values compromised. Both of these requires work, but not in the same way. Embracing and living values individually, and sharing them interpersonally, can be constructively nurtured and accomplished through various proactive and developmental approaches. Unfortunately, life is not always this straightforward and we may at any time run into a values conflict, the outcomes of which may often be unpredictable. For navigating through values conflicts we make a good start by being values-based and ethically minded, but we may also discover that this process entails mastery of a different kind for which we need courage, confidence and competence.

While we will attend to the upside of making values real in several chapters to follow, this one is about coming to terms with how we think, feel and act when faced with a values conflict. We will attend to the nature of values conflicts, the emotions that such conflicts evoke in us, the speaking up versus shutting up conundrums that we must work through, and the rationalisations that may confront us or tempt us to withdraw from it.

Much of our journey through this chapter connects with the work of Mary Gentile who has become world-renowned for her Giving Voice to Values (GVV) approach. There are a few basic premises to GVV that are of relevance for the journey that we are about to embark on. The first is that values conflicts, unsettling as they might be, are part of life and bound to occur in our relationships and workplaces. A values conflict may arise inasmuch in any seemingly ordinary conversation as in operational and transactional activities. In most of these situations, and this is the second premise, most people might know what the right thing is to do, but feel stuck, for various reasons, on how to get it done. The challenge is, therefore, to move beyond the awareness that something is morally unacceptable and the analysis of why that is the case to a place of action.[19] This brings us to a third and very hopeful premise, namely that we can develop the cognitive awareness, the moral confidence and the practical capabilities to deal with the variety of values conflicts that we are so often confronted with.

This book is about making values real and our focus is on processes that may help us to accomplish it. In this chapter it will be no different as we will blend three components together, namely Gentile's GVV approach, useful exercises for understanding and working with values conflicts and your own stories of values conflicts, whether past or present. I invite you to bring your whole self to the reading of this chapter and I hope that it will lead you to a better understanding of the dynamics involved in values conflicts.

Values in the red zone

I invite you to do a short exercise. Think about one or more recent situations of interactions with other people which sparked pleasant emotions for you. Situations in this case may refer to conversations, meetings, or events that you were a part of. Such situations may be located in your more informal domains of interacting with others or in more formal ones such as in the workplace or in transactional encounters. Pleasant emotions may include, among others, feelings of happiness, joy, contentment, gratitude and pride. Now go the opposite direction and identify situations of interaction with others which evoked unpleasant emotions in you, for example, anger, fear, anxiety, or disgust.

Once you have made these linkages – situations resulting in pleasant emotions on the one hand and those evoking unpleasant emotions on the other – you are ready for the next step. Revisit what these situations were about and who else were involved. What was said or what happened that aroused these emotions in you, whether pleasant or unpleasant? Now consider the possibility that your experience of at least some of these situations could be linked to one or more values upheld or violated. To be more specific, consider the potential connection between your pleasant and/or unpleasant experiences in different situations and how that might be related, for example, to a value such as honesty, respect, responsibility, fairness and/or compassion being either upheld or violated. If necessary, revisit chapter 2 and read again through the meaning of each of the five values as well as the observation about the pleasant outcomes of them being upheld and the unpleasant outcomes of them being neglected or violated. What insights do you come to?

The exercise you have just done is similar to what I do in values workshops by asking participants to capture recent experiences of interaction with others which left them with either happy or angry emotions. The happy ones are written up on yellow cards and the angry ones on red cards. Thereafter I introduce them to the working definition of values proposed in chapter 1, namely, the aspirational beliefs that we hold about human behaviours expressing how we prefer or agree to live and relate and determining what we regard as right or wrong in particular situations and the decisions we make as a result. This is followed by an invitation to share their happy and angry experiences as they might potentially relate to honesty, respect, responsibility, fairness and compassion either being upheld or violated. I usually make a poster of these five values available and recommend that they build a "heat map" of yellow and red cards as different experiences correspond to different values.

Apart from this exercise making the relationship between values and emotions tangible, it is also interesting to see how concentrations of yellow and red in relation to specific values might offer indications of good experiences and trouble spots when participants are from the same organisation. For example, in the case of one organisation I worked with, it was interesting to note how participants in management roles would have more red cards referring to honesty and responsibility, while employees with lesser authority would show more red cards around the values of respect, fairness and compassion. The message in their case seemed to be that managers tend to prioritise values linked to performance while employees were more sensitive about values relating to how they felt treated.

While I do not claim scientific rigour for this exercise, it does give reason for pause to reflect on the relationship between values and emotions. There is an extensive body of research on emotions as well as on emotions in relation to morality. While this discussion is not without controversy, I want focus on those views that are helpful for our purposes. Scarantino and de Sousa[20] state that "[n]o aspect of our mental life is more important to the quality and meaning of our existence than the emotions". They discuss three ways in which emotions have historically been conceptualised, namely, as distinctive conscious experiences, as evaluations of eliciting circumstances, and as motivations for behaviour. Without delving into their comprehensive critical discussion of these three traditions, it is worthy to note how they arrive at the conclusion that emotions are rational in cognitive and strategic ways. In terms of cognitive rationality, emotions refer to the ability to "represent the world as it is and properly relate to other evidence sensitive evaluative processes". Strategic rationality refers to the ability of emotions to "lead to actions that promote the agent's interests and properly relate to other action-influencing processes", for example decision-making.[21] We can, therefore, say that emotions are indicative and informative of how we experience, evaluate and react to different situations in life, including those with moral sensitivities.

Writing about the role of emotions in organisations, Frederickson[22] describes emotions as "multicomponent response tendencies" that begin with an individual's assessment of the personal meaning of some antecedent event. Positive emotions like joy, interest, pride, or contentment occur "when people feel safe and satiated". Negative emotions, such as anger, fear, anxiety, sadness "arouse people's automatic nervous systems, producing increases in heart rate, vasoconstriction, and blood pressure, among other changes". In a similar vein, and connecting it specifically to values, Bagozzi[23] refers to positive emotions as being associated with the attainment of a goal or subgoal resulting in feelings of excitement, happiness, and pride. Negative emotions, on the other hand, "result from problems with ongoing plans and failures to achieve desired goals, which can result in greater expenditure of effort, a change in plans, or even goal abandonment". Such emotions include anger, frustration, disappointment, shame, and worry.

When doing the happy - angry exercise in workshops I often notice with interest how participants can struggle to come up with yellow card experiences and how easily they produce a handful of red ones. It is noteworthy to reflect on why this is the case. It could be, as noted before, that we are simply less attentive to when things go well, and we experience harmony in our interactions with other. Our angry experiences, on the other hand, are more troublesome, experienced more intensely and therefore seem easier to remember.

Now that we have made the values - emotions connection, you can put your pleasant experiences to the side because for the rest of this chapter we will dig deeper into the nature of the unpleasant ones. Metaphorically speaking, we can say that we shift our attention now from the "yellow zone" of values-related emotions to the "red zone".

In the claws of a values conflict

David is the Head of Finance of a Public Sector institution. As is common with most public sector organisations, and especially the Head of Finance, a lot of weird and unnecessary demands are disguised as 'Orders from Above'. In his words, "you are expected to comply because it is an order. Or to be a little charitable, a request with veiled threats".

Because David's institution is financially well-resourced, a lot of demands are made on it from both the ministry and parliament and these demands come verbally, either through a phone call or during a meeting. He further explains that "as the supervisor of state funds, which are governed by many acts, it is difficult to part with any money without the necessary evidence in line with the laws". "In addition to that", he said, "the ethics of my profession, as well as my religious beliefs, bar me from engaging in any unethical behaviour. In the case of my profession, flouting the ethics comes with very punitive sanctions".

What made matters worse was that when the requests arrived, they were accompanied by advice on how the transaction can be consummated by using examples from other sister agencies. The purpose behind a request was mostly shrouded in secrecy, but some people were brazen enough to tell David that it was needed to support someone in a 'high authority'. "This is just to put the fear of God in you", he says. And so, David feels torn between the threat of losing his job, be transferred to a remote area, or adhering to the diabolic demands and suffer the possible consequences if reported.

"Thus far, I have succeeded in warding off the demands with a counter appeal to provide written requests for the funds, but it has come at a great cost in name-calling and other unprintable words." He knew it is a matter of time before things will boil over. He needs to find a solution for this wanton abuse of public funds which could have been used for other productive activities. More seriously, leaders who are obsessed with an inordinate desire for wealth will not allow anything to stand between them and their desires, even if it results in physical harm to others. "This is of extreme discomfort to me", he says.

It would be unrealistic to expect that we will always see eye to eye with others regarding the meaning and application of values in practice. However, there are two situations in which values conflicts occur that matter to our conversation in this chapter. The first is of a personal nature and, such as in David's case, involves experiences of either being treated badly or pressured to perform something that is in contrast to the values that we hold dear. The second is when we observe how others are being similarly treated or pressured. These situations can be as straightforward as experiencing or observing, for example, dishonesty, disrespect, irresponsibility, unfairness or lack of compassion. They can manifest as the violation of these values in situations of discrimination, exploitation, harassment, racism, sexism or nepotism, to name but a few. Or they might occur in concerns about pricing, quality, safety, bribery, fraud, tax evasion, copyright, waste, etcetera. Whether involving self or others, whether experienced or observed, situations such as these take us into the "red zone" of values conflict and require us to respond.

Rokeach[24] states that values have three components. The first, cognitive, refers to knowing "the correct way to behave or end-state to strive for". The second, affective, refers to the sense that a person may feel emotional about it, in other words, "approve of positive instances and disapprove of negative instances of it". The third, behavioural, "is an intervening variable that leads to action when activated". The yellow zone is where these three components generally function well together. What we know, feel and do in relation to living and voicing our values, are experienced as relatively unproblematic, even when it requires thoughtful consideration in relation to ourselves or in conversation or debate with others. In the "red zone" this synergy falls apart when knowing that something is wrong and feeling the displeasure that goes with it does not automatically translate into doing something about it. Why is the case?

One of the premises that we hold about values is that they are both personally internalised and relationally embedded. Where values are upheld in personal and relational terms, we benefit and enjoy multiple positive outcomes. Where values are violated, we are confronted with choice. We can confront the values conflict or walk away from it. Either way, there will be consequences. It is in this knowledge that the coherence of knowing-feeling-doing unravels and that speaking up, however much desired or expected, becomes a real challenge for many people.

Speaking up versus shutting up

By now you probably would have associated your "red zone" experience(s) with what it means to be confronted with a values conflict. Apart from the discomfort that one or more values are violated in situations involving you directly or observed by you in relation to others, you are challenged with choice. Have you done something about it, or not? If yes, why? If not, why not? Why is the choice between speaking up versus shutting up often so challenging?

Gentile[25] commits a whole chapter to what she calls "A Tale of Two Stories". This refers to a helpful exercise to work through the speaking up versus shutting up conundrum. The invitation in this exercise is to revisit and compare two what she calls "non-trivial" past experiences of values conflicts. The one experience must represent a situation in which the person spoke up and acted to resolve the conflict and the other must be one in which the person decided not to do so. The point of the exercise is to help people learn from their own values conflict experiences by comparing the situations involved and the reasons why they responded differently in each of the cases. Above all, it is also an exercise in self-discovery and moral strengthening when people discover that they were indeed able to voice their values effectively in certain situations, however difficult it might have been.

I invite you to apply the Tale of Two Stories exercise to a "red zone" experience in which you spoke up and acted and one in which you did not. Revisit both stories and first ask yourself what the situation was and who else was involved. Secondly, in the case of speaking up, what motivated you to speak up, what did you say or do, what were the outcomes and what could have made it easier for you to do so? In the case of not speaking up, what pushed you back, how did it turn out, and what could have made it easier for you to do so?

We may ask what kind of situations may represent values conflicts in which the choice between speaking up and shutting up becomes a real conundrum for people. Such situations may, among others, include any of the following: ordinary conversations, discussions and decisions in meetings, the appointment of staff or service providers, financial transactions and procedures, tenders and bidding processes, evaluations and reporting, and customer or community interactions. When faced with values conflicts in such situations, our default would be to say, speak up, stand your ground, do what is right and expose what is wrong. What I have learned from values conversations is that there are predominantly three factors at play that makes the difference between speaking up versus shutting up in values conflicts. Firstly, there is the question about who else is involved in the values conflict, secondly the motivation for speaking up or not and, thirdly, the leverage that we believe we have available to do so.

Regarding the "who else is involved" question, we may tend to be sensitive about our place and capacity for agency in the relationships involved around a values conflict. If we are senior to or having power over others and we are committed to values-driven action, speaking up is relatively straightforward. Caution and complexity steps in when "the other" are, for example, an authority, a senior, a colleague, or a friend one believes might be committing a values violation. The motivation for speaking up is often tied up with relational sensitivities and a sense of caution as people harbour fears and calculate risks, for example, sacrificing their position or job, being perceived and isolated as a troublemaker, or losing an important relationship. While often people would shy away from speaking up at this critical juncture, there are others who find leverage forthcoming from previous experiences, from seeking advice from trusted friends or mentors, and from doing their homework and becoming knowledgeable about the issues at stake in the values violations they are confronted with.

It is not difficult to admit that values conflicts are often tough to deal with. Sometimes we do act and speak up in values conflicts and sometimes we don't. When debriefing the Tale of Two Stories exercise, I often hear people saying, "pick your battles carefully". While this sounds like common wisdom, there is always the risk that shying away from addressing a values conflict might lead to more harm to others, to an organisation, or even society at large. On the other hand, there is also risk involved in taking a values conflict head on. While we may hope that we will be appreciated for voicing our values, there is always the possibility that we might suffer rejection by others, or ultimately by an organisation, as most whistleblowers are living examples of. It is not difficult to sense that in values conflicts we might feel like "damned if I do" and "damned if I don't". Either way there might be unpredictable outcomes. The question is whether we choose for living with regret or rather remain true to ourselves? It can be a tough corner to be in.

The severity of values violations varies, and so the complexity of the situations in which they occur. Many of us have our stories of choice between speaking up and shutting up. Many will admit to wearing the emotional and relational scars of taking on a values conflict or shying away from it. Ultimately, we may admit that shutting up lingers longer within us while speaking up builds our courage, confidence and competence over time. In Gentile's[26] words, we build "moral muscle" and "the habit of voicing our values". The values conversation is, therefore, not about human perfection or ethical superiority. It is rather about acknowledging that vulnerability, imperfection and fallibility are part of who we are and that choosing the path of voicing our values requires moral awareness, constant practice, learning from our mistakes and growing from our successes.

Reflect again on your Tale of Two Stories. What insights do you now have that you did not have before? What resonates with you regarding the three factors of context, motivation and leverage? Recalling context, who else was involved and why did that matter to you? As for motivation, what sensitivities, risks, or fears determined your decision to act or not in each of the stories? And reflecting on leverage, to what extent did your own sense of confidence and competence tripped you up or motivated you on to deal with the conflict?

So many excuses for not doing the right thing

The illustration below may help to further explain the speaking up versus shutting up conundrum. It works with the idea of a nested hierarchy in which the self with thoughts, feeling and judgments are linked into relationships of different kinds such as family, friends, colleagues, or fellow team members. Surrounding the previous are the community in which we live, the organisation which we work for, the society of which we are citizens, or the natural environment which we are dependent upon. A values conflict, as experienced or observed by self, is inevitably embedded in and consequential for the relationships at stake. It might even go further and involve the broader systems of embeddedness and interdependencies that we are a part of. Acting or not acting in a values conflict is inevitably consequential, and the repercussions of either are unpredictable.

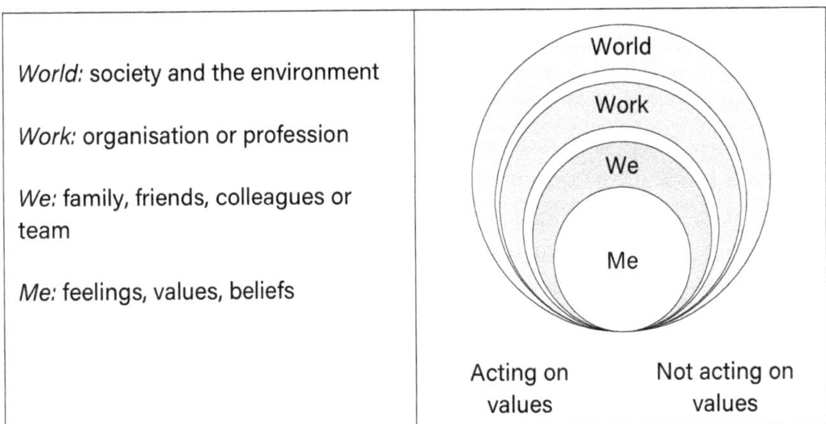

Figure 3.1: The me-we-work-world repercussions of a values conflict

The repercussions of the choice not to act, might remain limited and are only consequential for self, but it might allow harm to escalate to others and even have larger systemic consequences. While the choice for speaking up might be a truthful expression of what a person cares about, the appreciation thereof by others at the levels of we, work or world, cannot be taken for granted. Not speaking up might also leave us with the void of not knowing whether we would have been appreciated or supported by either those with whom we have specific relationships with or by the institutional structures, codes, or policies that we hope to rely on.

For the moment we will leave your "speaking up" story on the side and focus on the one in which you opted for not acting on your values. Looking back, you may realise that what held you back was not so much a matter of not knowing what the right thing was to do. Your avoidance of acting on your values might be due to the conundrum illustrated above. Combined with the desire to remain values-driven and ethical, there is some emotional and relational cost accounting at stake in values conflicts. This process brings us face to face with the phenomenon of rationalisations which in plain language means finding excuses for knowing but not doing the right thing. These excuses could either be located within us as we try to justify our withdrawal from uncomfortable values conflict, or it might be located in the attitudes and arguments of those that we try to confront about their values violations, or it might be more subtle and be embedded in the language and typical expressions of the organisations that we work for.

According to Gentile[27] there are four dominant rationalisations at work in organisations. "Common or standard practice" is the rationalisation referring to excuses based on what others seem to regard as a morally acceptable, even if ethically questionable. Should we then express our discomfort and confront someone about wrongdoing, we might be confronted with a form of self-justification that refers to the generally accepted, even expected, way in which things are being done. In my experience with workshop participants, they often associate this rationalisation with the example being set by those holding the power in the organisation and what they afford themselves as acceptable ways of operating. This kind of rationalisation easily becomes rooted in the culture of an organisation and becomes expressed in language such as "when in Rome you do as the Romans do". If the power-holders can bypass due process in appointments, accept facilitation fees as an inevitable cost for doing business, instruct others to misrepresent important information, to name a few, why then should they try to be different and go against the tide. Our story of David, the Head of Finance, certainly shows traces of this kind of rationalisation.

The second notable rationalisation is referred to as "materiality". The argument in this case is that the significance of an action is too small to matter or to hurt anyone. In organisations it often centres around resource abuse, referring to when people use that which is meant for the productive outputs of the organisation for their own benefit. It goes further when seemingly small exceptions to the rule are tolerated, for example, around appointments or procurement perceived to be too insignificant or urgent to follow due process. Temptations loom large when performance or financial reports or the credentials of a product are inflated in order to create a seemingly innocent positive impression of a certain state of affairs. These examples - and they can be multiplied - carry the message of something being "a minor issue", not worthy of being "fussed" about.

"Locus of responsibility" is the rationalisation offered to pass the buck or shift the blame. People using this excuse might present several reasons for not wanting to be kept accountable for a values violation. "This is not what I am paid to do" is just another way of saying that other people, for example management, or another department, should be kept accountable. They might plead ignorance or turn a blind eye to some wrong that happened under the watch of someone else. More so, they might tell you that nobody told them that something is morally unacceptable, or they might defend their behaviour by arguing they have never seen anybody getting in trouble for the same actions. This boils down to "I wash my hands in innocence" for something that I do not have stake in, that was not made clear to me, that the work of someone else is not my business, or that I cannot be kept accountable for what is not in my job description or line of work. Confronting this rationalisation might be met with a "mind your own business" attitude.

"Locus of loyalty" may be considered as one of the toughest rationalisations to deal with. It refers to situations of being caught between doing what is right and being loyal to people that we may have special relationships with. What do you do when a dear friend is misbehaving? How do you respond to a senior person expecting you to consider a family member for an appointment or a service provider to be prioritised in a bidding process? What if you become aware of someone, especially one with power, pursuing private interests that might undermine the organisation that you work for? What if a senior is untruthful with respect to information or disrespectful in talking to or about others? Confronting these misguided expressions of loyalty might be met with "don't expect me to put my job on the line", or "I am only trying to be helpful", or "if I do not look after myself, who else will?" Back to David, the Head of Finance, again, he could, if not standing strong, be tempted into internalising this rationalisation.

It is important to note that rationalisations, in relation to values, act like defence mechanisms. Rokeach[28] refers to values as "multifaceted standards that guide our conduct in a variety of ways". Among these are that we use values to present ourselves as we evaluate, and judge, and apportion praise and blame on ourselves and others. We also employ values as standards to compare our morality and competence to that of others on the basis of which we might also decide which beliefs, attitudes, values and actions of others "are worth challenging, protesting, and arguing about, or worth trying to influence or to change". Rokeach further argues that "values are standards that tell us how to rationalise in the psychoanalytic sense, beliefs, attitudes and actions that would otherwise be personally and socially unacceptable so that we may end up with personal feelings of morality and competence". Ironic as it appears, this is an important point to understand, namely that rationalisations, misguided as they might be, are attempts at maintaining self-esteem. We should, therefore, not only be attentive to the rationalisations of others but also to our own. The same rationalisations that others might push back with when confronted in a values conflict, we might be tempted to use for avoiding discomfort and refraining from speaking up. Rationalisations remind us that the moral discomfort that is aroused in us in the "red zone" does not automatically translate into speaking up in defence of the very same values that we experience to be confronted.

Rationalisations seldom hunt alone

Consider the following story. A young doctor at a primary care clinic, seeing 50-60 patients per day, is experiencing tremendous strain as he attempts to fulfil his responsibility of quality patient care. Patients only get to spend a few minutes with the busy doctor. To make matters worse, clinical nurse practitioners continue to refer patients from the "sick lines" even though they are stable and can be scheduled appropriately or can simply be discussed with the doctor. The doctor also has academic demands on his time but cannot get to them due to the sheer number of patients, often skipping lunch, tea or bathroom breaks. The operational manager also experiences various pressures regarding staffing and the provincial health department's "ideal clinic" initiative. This initiative is, among other things, about clinics with good infrastructure, adequate staff, adequate medicine and supplies, and good administrative processes. An ideal clinic furthermore abides by applicable clinical policies, protocols and guidelines while also harnessing partner and stakeholder support.

There is an obvious gap between this doctor's lived experience and the espoused ideals of his healthcare environment. Listening to his story at a values workshop for healthcare practitioners, one could sense his emotional state. He felt overwhelmed, disillusioned, frustrated, angry and lonely. Several values were at stake for him as he felt the weight of responsibility towards patients, other staff members and the healthcare system. He was wondering about fairness toward the patients whom he could not afford sufficient time to see and treat properly. And he was wondering about fairness toward himself regarding a workload that pushed him to the limits.

Given his obvious predicament amid this untenable situation, one might ask about what kept him from speaking up. This is where the rationalisations started to show up. He felt young and not eligible to speak up. He wanted to show strength and avoid being regarded as not being good or tough enough to work under such strenuous circumstances. Furthermore, he felt dependent on the goodwill of senior doctors – for his career's sake – and that of nursing staff so that they will not overload him even more. On the flipside, he identified the prevailing rationalisations in the system. He expected the standard practice argument to be that this is just the way things are, and the plight of a young doctor is to do his bit for the sake of the system and to secure his career. He could sense a locus of responsibility rationalisation prevalent among nursing staff who only took responsibility for stocking the "sick line" without regard for the policies and procedures that support quality healthcare and fair work allocations. And within himself he wrestled with whether his own well-being is material enough to make an issue of. Rationalisations seldom hunt alone; they often become systemically pervasive.

This story encapsulates so much of what we have discussed in this chapter. While pinned on the values conflicts experienced by one person, there appears to be a whole host of other role players involved, namely other doctors, nursing and administrative staff, and patients. More distantly and indirectly there are also stakeholders who oversee the functioning of the healthcare bureaucracy via policies and procedures. The story cuts through the whole me-we-work-world diagramme (figure 3.1). There is no question about the emotional state of the doctor, how he finds himself caught between speaking up or shutting up. For an observer the temptation might be to view this as either a failure of personal courage on the doctor's side or a lack of operational savvy in the system. Neither argument will comfort the young doctor or satisfy the patients, or the wider public for that matter, in the event that his predicament might lead to bad clinical judgement and life risk for a patient. Should this happen, he will most likely feel even more abandoned.

The young doctor was reluctant to speak up until he attended a values workshop. What then happened, we will come back to later.

What can we learn from values conflicts?

We are only halfway through our exploration of values conflicts. The better part, namely the possibility of resolving them, will be tackled in the next chapter. For now, I want to reflect on three insights emerging from the discussion thus far. The first is that it is a common human experience that along the journey of life we will be frequently confronted with values conflicts and the choice between speaking up versus shutting up. It is in these moments that we experience how human interactions, uncomfortable emotions and the values we desire to adhere to become all up bundled up together. A values conflict is not just about rational choice. It becomes an embodied experience. It burns energy.

Secondly, if we listen carefully, we will notice rationalisations surprisingly frequently. It pops up in the language of our interpersonal and workplace encounters. "I am only doing what I have been told to do." "Mind your own business." "This is not what I get paid for." "This is someone else's problem." "Why will I stick my neck out?" "I do not want to be a pain." "I am new here." "I have told management many times." "There will be no risk to consumers." "Don't single me out." "I just followed due process." "The problem it too big." "We do not have time for this now." "We have always done it like this." "The agenda is closed." "Let's refer it to a committee." While it might be important to know the specifics of a situation before judging it as a values conflict, there is good reason to be attentive to expressions such as these. When in doubt, rather regard them as signals for values conflicts and potential rationalisations.

Lastly, the realisation that a rationalisation exists may become the first step towards engagement with a values conflict. A few years ago, I led a director development programme, starting with a module on values-driven leadership. The programme ran over three modules separated by a month in between. At the start of the second module one of the participants arrived beaming with excitement. He said to me, "You know what, in board meetings I can now hear the rationalisations as they build up in discussions and I am ready to tackle them!" What this readiness means, is what we will explore next.

Conclusion

Being confronted with a values conflict is more than just an unpleasant experience. It involves risk. Acting and speaking up preserve and build personal authenticity and integrity and may translate into positive outcomes for our relationships, and for the organisations and societies that we are members of. However, we may also experience criticism and even rejection for having done so. This risk should not deter us, but can we find a way to achieve both objectives at the same time? Yes we can, even if not in all situations. How this is possible, it the focus of the next chapter.

It is time for your journal again. While reading this chapter, I assume that you were able to recall at least one experience of a values conflict that you were challenged by. While being in this "red zone, which considerations did you go through regarding acting versus not acting on your values? What did you identify as the consequences of acting versus not acting? And in choosing for not acting, were you able to recognise one or more rationalisations? How were these rationalisations expressed? What behaviours did you observe? What language was used? What rationalisations were you harbouring within yourself?

Now consider the following questions:

- What have you learned about your default tendencies for dealing with values conflicts? Are you more inclined to deal with them or do you rather prefer to shy away from them?
- What is most challenging for you about speaking up and acting on your values?
- If you harbour any dominant scripts that tend to withhold you from dealing with values conflicts, how would you phrase them? What will it take to change these scripts?
- In values conflicts that you come up against, for example, at work, what rationalisations are you now able to identify? What is the language in which they are expressed?

CHAPTER 4

VALUES UPHELD

> What if you were going to act on your values - what would you say and do?
>
> —*Mary Gentile*

INTRODUCTION

A friend of mine taught me to "let the question be our teacher". We do have a guiding question for this book: How can we make values real? Thus far, following this question has paid off for us. The question helped us to profile values within a broader constellation of concepts. It took us into an in-depth exploration of a handful of core values. It also brought us face to face with why we at times try to rationalise our way out of the discomfort of values conflicts. In this chapter, following the question will lead us to considering ways in which we might best succeed in resolving values conflicts constructively and ethically. In the process, the skill of raising good questions will become a central topic of our discussion. A well-considered question is often the first step towards getting the yeast of values working in a values conflict.

Rescripting as a method and skill for dealing with values conflicts will be at the heart of this chapter. We will explore what rescripting is about and how to apply it in practice.

Rescripting interacts with the rationalisation scripts with the intention of transforming them into reasons for doing the right thing. The good news is that rescripting can be practiced and mastered and therefore also become a habituated behaviour in difficult conversations.

Keep your "red zone" story in mind as we work through this chapter. At the end you will be invited to plot it out on a framework that you will be introduced to, namely the Giving Voice to Values Canvas.

Speaking up and surviving it

A participant in values workshop once shared a fascinating story. The background is a board meeting of a company that he at the time was a director of. Not only was this his first meeting with this board; he was also the most junior one among the board members. The culture was one of rank and seniority and you had to wait your turn and earn the right to speak. Amid all this caution there was an agenda item that he felt much discomfort about. The board had to decide on the appointment of a contractor that he believed would not be in the best interests of the organisation. He also had a suspicion that there were conflicts of interest at stake which could not be exposed and confronted without risk. He had a choice between knowing his place and leave the decision to the senior board members or speaking up and doing so at the risk of being marginalised within the board. Speaking up also held the risk of putting his personal safety at risk in public. He explained to us how he navigated his participation in the discussion by means of three questions. The first was about whether this contractor was appointed before. Upon receiving confirmation, his second question was about whether the board was satisfied with the contractor's performance. The debate that followed exposed opposing opinions among the other board members. He then posed his third question: Shall we appoint the contractor again?

It is not difficult to imagine the rationalisations that might have been at work in the story above. The junior director seemed to have been up against at least two rationalisations, namely standard practice or locus of loyalty considerations. If it was about standard practice, he might have been faced with how appointments of this nature have always been made, namely that the authority and preferences of senior decision makers overrides proper duo diligence. If locus of loyalty was the rationalisation at stake, some people might have offered their personal acquaintance with the contractor as their argument in favour of appointing while masking the personal benefits that they might derive from such an arrangement. On the junior director's side of the story, he could bow before the force of authority and the existing way of doing things. He could also opt for protecting his position on the board and his dependence on the income and reputation that he could earn from it. What he did instead, was to turn the discussion around with three wisely scripted questions and save the board, and the company, the reputational damage that may have resulted from an unwise appointment. Part of the beauty of this story for me was that this person was not consciously rescripting as a result of attending the values workshop. He brought a story of his own into our discussions from which we all could learn what rescripting a values conflict can accomplish. Without consciously knowing it, this director followed the way of the baker: he mixed the yeast of values into the dough of a difficult conversation and achieved a surprising outcome.

Contrary to rationalisations that present reasons for not dealing with a values conflict, rescripting is about finding reasons for actively engaging with it. As with rationalisations, Gentile remains our guide for understanding what rescripting amid a values conflict is about. The central thesis of her GVV approach is to shift the question from what the right thing is to do to how to get the right thing done. While remaining anchored in a values-based position in the midst of a values conflict, rescripting is about developing arguments for constructive engagement with those we have the values conflict with. To achieve this turnaround, Gentile[29] proposes that we work through a sequence of questions, starting with the action or decision that we believe is right and working from there to consider the main arguments against the rationalisations that one would likely encounter. In these arguments we would find the rationalisations we may need to address. If we keep in mind that rationalisations point toward interests, needs or fears which might be at stake for the parties involved – others and ourselves – we are more ready to develop persuasive arguments for getting the right thing done. Having gone through this path of reasoning we may move on to considering with whom, when and in what context the argument for right action could best be made.

If we take the four most frequently used rationalisations, as discussed in the previous chapter, through a rescripting process, this is broadly what we would aim for:

- If the rationalisation for justifying unethical behaviour is anchored in *standard practice* (the generally accepted way of doing things), the aim would be to develop a counter argument and initiate a conversation around *best practice*, in other words, standards that express the best behaviours and actions that stakeholders in the situation are capable of.
- Should *materiality* (small impact, little risk of harm) be at the heart of a rationalisation, then a counter argument could be developed on the grounds of *transparency*, prompting consideration of those for whom a decision, action or behaviour might indeed be harmful as well as highlighting the consequences of it becoming publicly known.
- If we happen to deal with a *locus of responsibility* rationalisation (the problem is for someone else to care about), the rescripting argument could be built on the repercussions of not taking *action* as well as the development of *solutions* to correct the situation.
- In facing up to a locus of loyalty rationalisation (caught between competing interests or relationships) the counter argument could push for depersonalising the conflict by introducing a level of objectivity through which the other party could be swayed from a choice between competing loyalties to considering what following a fair process or procedure might be like.

While the above seems helpful and logical, the question is how such shifts can be accomplished. The key lies in developing an alternative script to guide the engagement in a values conflict with. Gentile refers to the development of counter arguments as pre-scripting. With that she refers to a written process in which we develop alternative scripts for engaging with values conflicts. For developing effective scripts, Gentile[30] recommends careful reflection on the following questions: "What is the action or decision that we believe is right? What are the main arguments against this course that we're likely to encounter? What are the reasons and rationalisations we will need to address? What's at stake for the key parties, including those who disagree with us? And what's at stake for us? What are our most powerful and persuasive responses to the reasons and rationalisations we need to address? To whom should the argument be made? When and in what context?"

A story of collusion

Let's take a rescripting journey with George. He is the Chief Administrative and Academic Officer of an academic institution. It came to his attention that 65 out of 110 students fairly failed a course in their second year, eight of whom then colluded with examination officers to alter their grades in the examination management system. Some IT personnel were also involved in this act. By the time of the discovery, these students were already in the first semester of their final year. George was understandably shocked and regarded this as one of the biggest ethical dilemmas he has ever faced. What must he do with these students? What about the credibility of his university if the matter goes public? How could his own staff, the examination officers, not strictly abide by the university's examination policy? Why has there been a systems failure to detect the alteration of marks for so long?

George found himself amid a values conflict. His university's values, namely, diligence, integrity honesty and quality consciousness, were at stake. In as much as he subscribes to the same values, he also felt his leadership capabilities to be under scrutiny – a very sensitive matter in his area of responsibility escaped his attention. His own staff explained that they just wanted to be helpful as the eight students under discussion were all borderline cases by missing between one and three marks to pass. Meanwhile he learned that some other students were aware of the situation, and they were planning to report the matter to the corruption bureau.

Rationalisations abound in this story. George seems to battle with locus of loyalty. Should he follow due process as dictated by policy, and the matter becomes public, there is no guarantee that he will be honoured for his leadership. His team members seem to pin their actions on the argument of materiality and justify it with "we just wanted to be helpful". We know little of the motivations of the IT staff, but they would most likely argue that they could not be held responsible for what they were told to do, namely, to change the marks. The eight students, one could speculate, were exploiting weak spots in the system and leveraging some personal relationships within George's department, as well as copying behaviours that other students before them might have gotten away with.

George's rescripting process will have to start with himself, and he seems ready for it, namely, to rise above his personal predicament, depersonalise the situation, and honour both the values and policies of his institution. However, having made this choice, there are several other rationalisations to deal with. What must he do with the eight students? Does he warn them, penalise them or expel them? How will he respond if they tell him that collusive practices in the institution are more widespread than what he might be aware of, and that they are not going to take it lightly if singled out for their transgression? What must he do with his staff? Should he just accept their good intentions, educate them about the risky consequences of apparently insignificant actions and let them get away with a warning? Or should he prime deeper and establish if there is not more to their relationships with these eight students than what meets the eye? What is the potential of them being caught up in locus of loyalty conundrums within and beyond the institution? IT reports to another line manager, but their complicity and lack of procedural correctness cannot be excused. How will he approach this conversation with another manager who might tell him to mind his own business? What does it point to if 65 out of 110 students fail a course? Could there perhaps be shortcomings in teaching and assessment practices that must be investigated? And if the latter is the case, he will have to engage with the academic staff in the department concerned more widely. With this group he might have to face up to what they accept as their established standards of teaching and assessment and try to bring them around to participate in what can produce better academic outcomes.

If George gets the rescripting process right, he might be able to address not only the immediate values conflict through a narrow strategy focused on the students only, but to embark on a systemically wholesome intervention process that may restore values consciousness and commitment on a wider scale among various stakeholders. When I use this and other stories in training workshops, we never start with an early verdict premised on a single-minded solution. We always start with understanding the situation and the stakeholders involved. Then we walk with the protagonist through their feelings, the values at stake for them and their judgement of what they would regard as the right thing to do.

Thereafter we explore the speaking up vs shutting up consequences at the levels of me-we-work-world as an introduction to how the protagonist might respond to the rationalisations that different stakeholders would tender for not doing the right thing or not being willing to be confronted for not doing so. Then the scene is set for articulating possible scripts that the protagonist might use to pursue a values-driven outcome.

Conversations as rescripting spaces

In the previous chapter, I promised to bring the young doctor back into the discussion. At the workshop where he shared his story, he ended up in a small working group consisting of very experienced healthcare professionals, particularly nursing sisters. They have seen this kind of situation before. Having listened with empathy to his burden, they navigated him through a rescripting process that empowered him for a conversation with the nursing and administrative staff of the clinic where he works. They confirmed that patients can be differentiated between those who must see the doctor and those who only need the attention of the nursing staff. The locus of responsibility rationalisation can therefore be shifted towards an agreed upon action plan. Furthermore, the administrative processes can be changed to fit the standards of the ideal clinic protocols; there was no reason for staff to defend a sub-standard status quo. As a result of this conversation, the doctor was able to reclaim the healthcare values that he stood for. He got his voice back. His juniority was no longer a liability and he could stand up, speak up and drive an essential change. While the solution seems so operational, this kind of situation only needs one patient to suffer unnecessarily, or even die, as a result of negligent healthcare for it to be branded as a major ethical failure.

The values workshop in which the young doctor participated, was part of a series of workshops led by me and two medical doctors in a public healthcare district over a period of four years, the time of the Covid pandemic included. When the strict lockdown was lifted and we were able to run in-person workshops again, we became aware of the rationalisations that healthcare professional had to face from people who were resistant to taking vaccines. This created and uncomfortable experience for healthcare workers already overburdened by the pandemic's impact while being at the same time also concerned about their own health and safety and that of their families. We realised that reprimanding and convincing the so-called anti-vaxxers was mostly counter-productive and led to more resistance than anything else. Instead, we argued that a more effective approach would be to help them come to an informed decision about vaccination. By bringing a values-driven angle to the problem, we opted in favour of a rescripting-based conversation format.

We observed how values were ingrained in the arguments that vaccine hesitant individuals were prone to put forward. Starting with honesty, many were not trusting the information about vaccination that was availed to them and tended to view their vaccination status as a private matter. Arguments around respect showed up with those who felt they were treated as guinea pigs in a new vaccination regime of which the outcomes, according to them, have not been conclusively tested and proven. The value of responsibility was at stake in conversations where some claimed that they would take care of themselves as long as others will do the same. Some felt that it was not fair to expect from them to be vaccinated for the sake of others' health and safety. Notions of compassion were present when arguments were put forward around love for self and/or family, thereby avoiding the risks that vaccination might hold for them.

One may now ask about the rationalisations and rescripting involved in such vaccine hesitancy conversations. We (North, Smit & Jenkins)[31] published an article in which we presented some rationalisations and how they might be rescripted as summarised in the table below.

Table 4.1: Rescripting rationalisation in vaccine hesitancy conversations (Adapted from North, Smit & Jenkins[32]

Rationalisations	**Rescripting possibilities**
Standard practice: The argument may be that many others, even experts, also do not trust the vaccines and therefore there was no reason to be different to them.	Ask about sources of information that the person trusts most, what they know thus far about the vaccines and what may help them to come to a well-informed decision. Also ask about the kind of information that could give the person confidence to consider vaccination.

Rationalisations	**Rescripting possibilities**
Materiality: A person may argue that them not being vaccinated will not make any difference, that herd immunity will in any case happen, or that they are sufficiently isolated to not be of risk to anybody.	The conversation could include questions that may help a person see the bigger picture of themselves in relation to others. Inquire about the relevance to them of knowing someone else's Covid or vaccine status and whether others would appreciate knowing theirs too.
Locus of responsibility: A person may argue that the safety of the vaccines and the provision of risk-free healthcare are for others to care about as long as they are left alone to take care of themselves and manage their own risk.	In this scenario, a reflection on personal responsibility may be helpful. Inquire about the person's concerns for family, friends, colleagues' or healthcare workers' safety and the precautions expected from them. Ask about how the person might best act in the interest of self and the people they care about.
Locus of loyalty: With this rationalisation someone could argue that their loyalty was to self and family, not to those (government or big pharma) who pushed for vaccinations.	This scenario calls for a conversation about the person's significant relationships. Inquiry could be made about the people that matter most to them, how they would like to relate to them, and what would be helpful for them to have the most connected, natural and safest interaction with them. In addition, they could be asked about the role that them being vaccinated can play in normalising these precious relationships.

Referring to the Covid-19 pandemic, the above feels far removed from us now. It may even be argued that these recommendations are limited to consulting room conversations. However, pandemic type conditions might return, and we'll be having similar conversations all over again. At the same time, the illustration above is not dissimilar to values conflicts that we may be challenged with in other contexts, some more severe than others. What is to be noted is the principle lying at the heart of the rescripting process, namely conversations that are not based on enforcing our own views onto others but meeting them where they are. This requires that we uphold their dignity even if we differ from them. It also requires that we make an effort of understanding their position and related challenges so that we may know what is at stake for them. Lastly it requires that we carefully prepare ourselves to work through a values conflict and its related rationalisations by developing counter arguments that may lead to values-driven outcomes.

The above illustrates an important aspect of our leading metaphor. Yeast, taken directly from its container and being thrown into the bread baking ingredients does not activate anything. Carefully prepared under the right conditions before being mixed into the dough allows the yeast to do its fermenting work most effectively. We should rather not use values as conversation stoppers, or as blunt expressions of that which we are against. It is better to view them as mediators towards ethical conversations and decision outcomes. The questions we ask play an important role in achieving this ideal.

The power of questions

I started the chapter by referring to my friend's constant reminder: "let the question be our teacher". Questions can be asked in many ways. Some are open; others are closed. Some are threatening; others are inviting. Some probe for information; others seek understanding. All types of questions can teach us something, but my friend's "teacher questions" are about open and non-threatening invitations to conversations that improve understanding. Questions in a values conflict should ideally not be like an interrogation in a lawsuit, but more like an invitation to explore better pathways for getting the right thing done.

Broadly speaking, there are three categories of questions at stake here. The first refers to the kind of questions that we may ask to enable rescripting, in other words to shift rationalisations into reasons for doing the right thing. These we have sufficiently dealt with in previous sections of this chapter. The second category is about the questions we may ask ourselves when caught up in a values conflict and are trying to find a way for dealing with it. This I will address in the last section. The third refers to questions that may help us to prepare for engaging in a values conflict and this is what our focus will be on next.

Plump[33] recommends the consideration of five factors for the process of preparing a script to tackle a values conflict with. Below is an adapted version of her presentation, each introduced by a leading question:

- *Who are the intended audience for your script?*: It makes a difference whether the audience is a single person or many, or even a department or whole organisation. Furthermore, knowing your audience will help you understand the interests, issues and values that are at stake for them. In preparation, you may even need to have consultative meetings before addressing your intended audience.
- *What will be the best communication approach to follow?*: You may need to choose between communicating in person or in writing. If in person, you may need to choose between a virtual and a face-to-face meeting. If face to face, you have to think about the most conducive place to meet. Time might also be a factor in choosing your communication style, medium and or place. If the matter is urgent and time is of the essence your communication choices may differ from when it is not the case.
- *What information or data do you need?*: Preparation is about gaining all relevant information about the issue under consideration. Inquiry might be about, among other things, the frequency of occurrence of the values conflict at stake, knowledge about the role players involved, and/or existing policies or procedures relevant to dealing with the situation.
- *How complex is the situation?*: If the scale of impact of a situation is limited, the engagement with it might involve a small number of people. However, if the scale of impact is big, the approach to dealing with it might involve several stakeholders and several interrelated factors to consider. In the case of the latter, a multi-stage approach should rather be considered.
- What are the risks at stake?: Risks, in the case of voicing your values, may include retaliation, being demoted, fired or marginalised, and physical, mental or professional harm. Risks in the case of not voicing your values may lead to continued harm to others, or the organisation involved, and the perpetuation of the conditions that caused the values conflict in the first place.

An iterative process

Working through some values conflicts may turn out to be relatively straightforward. However, taking the dynamics that are often present into account, it can also be experienced as challenging and complex. It is seldom a linear or stepwise process; it is rather more iterative. In a values workshop with healthcare professionals a surgeon expressed his profession's preference for a stepwise procedure to reach conclusions about a diagnosis or treatment. My response was that some values conflicts might indeed be solved on the spot but in many cases we have to go around the proverbial block more than once in order to arrive at an answer that we feel confident to work with. At the end of the workshop, the surgeon raised his hand again, smiling and admitting that an iterative approach seems indeed more appropriate.

What does such an iterative approach look like? To work through a values conflict, I propose the use of what I refer to as the Giving Voice to Values Canvas (figure 4.1). The GVV Canvas can be used as a guide to work through a values conflict to arrive at a feasible plan of action. Guided by the canvas, we may look at it as a process in four stages, namely 1) the awareness and assessment of the situation, 2) the understanding of the conflict and rationalisations at stake, 3) the re-scripting process and available resources to develop arguments for doing the right thing, and 4) the development of an action plan for engagement.

In view of these four stages or blocks of work to be done in working through a values conflict, there are a number of helpful questions to reflect on. Confronted by a values conflict, these are the question you may consider while using the GVV Canvas as a guide:

Stage 1: Awareness and assessment of the situation

In a values conflict, it is wise to come to a thorough understanding of the situation and the other role players involved, to connect with the feelings you have about it, to consider the values at stake and the assumptions that you hold about right and wrong regarding the situation. Considering the following questions, will assist in this process:

- What is causing the values conflict and who are the people involved?
- What do I feel about this situation? Why do I feel this way?
- What value(s) do I consider confronted in the situation?

Stage 2: The conflict, repercussions and rationalisations at stake

Confronted with a values conflict, it is advisable to work through the me-we-work-world framework to determine the repercussions of acting vs not acting on your values. Understanding your own position in the face of a values conflict prepares you for dealing with the rationalisations that you may have to confront, those of others as well as your own. Identifying and understanding those rationalisations, as expressed in speech, attitudes and behaviours, prepares you for the rescripting process to follow. The following questions, may lead to helpful insights:

- What action or decision do I believe is right? What stands in my way of getting it done?
- What may the consequences be for me, my relationships, organisation or society if I act or not act to address the values conflict?
- What rationalisations, those of others and those of myself, may I need to address?
- If there are multiple rationalisations, which are they and who holds which rationalisations?
- What interests are tied up in those rationalisations and what is at stake for those holding them?

Stage 3: Resources for rescripting and action

Rationalisations may abound, depending on the situation and stakeholders involved. The intention with this very important stage in the process is to make sure that you do not only address the right audience and issue(s) at stake, but that you also possess of relevant information and data to build the argument(s) that you want to put forward. It is important to prepare for a conversation in language that those whom you plan to engage in the values conflict can connect with and understand. Authentic engagement also includes the self-knowledge and experience that you bring to the situation. The important questions to ask during this part of the process are the following:

- What rationalisation(s) must be countered? With what script(s) can I counter the rationalisation(s)? What argument(s) will work best to make my new script(s) effective?
- Whom can I seek advice from? What information, research, standards, policies or codes can I make use of?
- What do I bring to the situation in terms of values, previous experiences, knowledge, or skills?

Stage 4: Concluding reflections and action plan for engagement

Although we refer to four stages, it should be kept in mind that we are dealing here with an iterative process through which we build preparation for action and engagement. This being confirmed, there is a reflective transition between the preceding work and the readiness for action. This readiness implies several important choices to be made regarding audience, time, place and method. Reflecting on the following questions, may bring the necessary clarity for stepping towards action:

- What insights am I gaining that may strengthen my resolve for a values-driven response?
- What will I do next? With whom, when, where, and how will I take this action?

A few notes on the structure of the GVV Canvas may be helpful. The centre of the canvas represents a situation with a protagonist and other stakeholders involved. To the left, the situation is linked with the protagonist's emotions about it and to the right with the values that the protagonist regards to be in conflict. Upwards from the situation is the protagonist's conflict experience, linked to the left with the repercussions of acting vs not acting and to the right with the rationalisations standing in the way of a values-driven response. Downwards from the situation is a reflective process sitting in-between the rescripting option and the resources available to the protagonist. At the bottom, there is space for considering an action plan for steering the values conflict toward a values-driven outcome.

Giving Voice to Values Canvas

Repercussions: What may the consequences be for me, my relationships, organisation or society if I act or not act to address the values conflict?

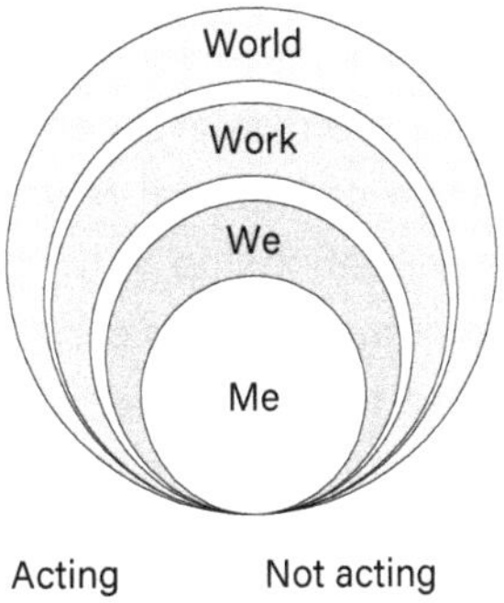

World
Work
We
Me

Acting | Not acting

The conflict: What action or decision do I believe is right? What stands in my way of getting it done?

Rationalisations: What rationalisations, those of others and those of myself, may I need to address? If there are multiple rationalisations, which are they and who holds which rationalisations? What interests are tied up in those rationalisations and what is at stake for those holding them?

Standard practice	Materiality
Locus of responsibility	Locus of loyalty

Emotions: What do I feel about this situation? Why do I feel this way?

The situation: What is causing the values conflict and who are the people involved?

Values: What value(s) do I consider confronted in the situation?

Rescripting: What rationalisation(s) must be countered? With what script(s) can I counter the rationalisation(s)? What argument(s) will work best to make my new script(s) effective?

Standard practice: What might best practice look like?	Materiality: For whom does it matter? What if it becomes public?
Locus of responsibility: What corrective action could be taken?	Locus of loyalty: What could be a fair process to follow?

Reflections: What insights am I gaining that may help me develop a values-driven response?

Resources: What do I bring to the situation in terms of values, previous experiences, knowledge, or skills? Whom can I seek advice from? What information, research, standards, policies or codes can I make use of?

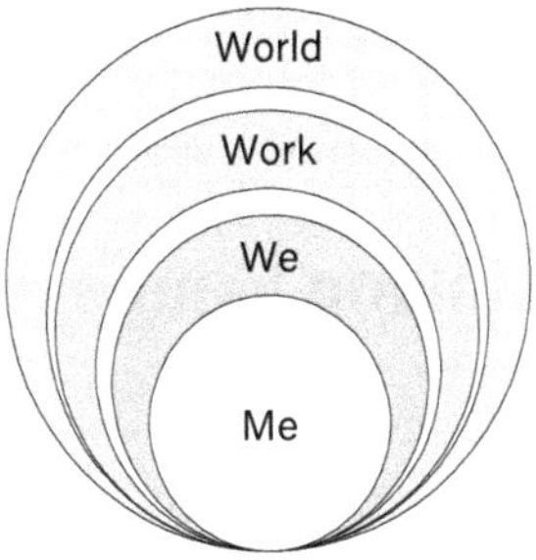

World
Work
We
Me

Action: What will I do no next? With whom, when, where, and how will I take this action?

Figure 4.1: The Giving Voice to Values Canvas

You may well ask whether there is value in using the GVV Canvas. When I developed my course materials for values workshops, I consulted with a concept artist who has also a very good understanding of effective learning processes. Once the canvas was completed, he asked me if I was willing to be a guinea pig for testing the framework. I was eager to do so, and he asked me whether I may think of a values conflict that was bothering me. Incidentally, I was struggling with one at the time. The situation was in brief about an honorarium for work that I have done for an organisation. There was no invoice involved, only a promise of a certain amount. I was confident that I deserved some form of financial reward but cautious to ask, fearing that it could put my relationship with the organisation at risk. As he guided me through the elements of the canvas, I realised that I was harbouring some anger linked to an experience of unfairness. My speaking up versus shutting up conundrum was about the dependency that I experienced in the relationship, knowing that if I don't speak up, I will forfeit the honorarium and lose my trust in the people involved. At the same time, I was quite apprehensive about what speaking up would do to our working relationship going forward. I was, in fact, harbouring a rationalisation within myself, one which was anchored in locus of loyalty considerations. Once I realised that, the rescripting part fell open for me as I was then able to shift my focus from the relational binds that I experienced to a process-based conversation at an upcoming meeting. Going into that meeting with a non-anxious and well-prepared question, the matter was easily resolved with no relational consequences in the aftermath. With this story I am not claiming that the canvas-based process that I recommend will be a panacea for all values conflicts, but I have found that it ever since has worked for many other people in working through their values conflicts.

Making values real

How do we make values real? Part of the answer is that values are real. Values are present in every conversation, meeting, or transaction. Values are present in our attitudes, decisions, and behaviours. When we are in the "yellow zone" of "happy" encounters, we may not even think about the presence of values. When we are in the "red zone" of "angry" encounters, the presence and experience of values become tacit in uncomfortable ways. Making values real amid a values conflict is for many of us a challenging undertaking.

When faced with a values conflict, it may help to keep a few helpful tips in mind. First of all, remember that values are because we are, that values count because we are interrelated, that coming to values agreements is something that we need to work on, and that values conflicts are bound to occur because of our human imperfections and fallibility. If we understand this, we realise that values are ever-present and that values conflicts are not exceptional occurrences.

Secondly, the good news is that values conflicts, however challenging and uncomfortable they often seem to be, are not unresolvable. We are capable of growing in confidence and competence to work through values conflicts and bring them to actionable outcomes. This chapter, in combination with the previous one, showed us a process-based and iterative pathway that can be followed. When faced with a values conflict, whether large or small, reflect on the questions recommended in the previous section and plot your thoughts onto the canvas. Follow the principle of the yeast and allow your reflections to mature. Use the resources at your disposal and work your way toward an action plan that you are confident to follow.

Thirdly, the process-based pathway recommended in this chapter is not just for dealing with the negative side of values conflicts. Over time it may also provide an empowering pathway towards growing personal, relational and organisational capacity for positive values-driven behaviour. In post-workshop evaluations I have found that participants have come to a better understanding of the ever-present nature of values in their lives and relationships, whether at home, at work or in society in general. They feel better equipped to engage in values conversations and to overcome the barriers that previously shield them away from dealing with values conflicts. They find the rescripting process particularly helpful as it gives them tools for transitioning from the disempowering impact of rationalisations to values-driven action plans with potentially constructive outcomes for themselves and others.

Conclusion

This chapter was in a certain way a culmination of the first four chapters of the book. In chapter 1, we did conceptual housekeeping by discussing values in relation to ethics, virtues and rules. In chapter 2, we delved deeper into the presence, meaning and interrelatedness of five common values in our everyday existence, whether in personal, relational, organisational or societal settings. In chapters 3, we focused on the nature of values conflicts and why it appears to be so challenging for us to get them resolved. In this chapter we argued that our values can be upheld in values conflicts and thereby lead to positive outcomes for ourselves and others.

Mastering rescripting is a big step in the direction of upholding our values amid the many challenges and conflicts we are so regularly confronted with. However, it is not the full story yet. In the next chapter we will focus on several helpful practices through which we can nurture our capacity for values-driven agency in our spheres of influence and responsibility. It will be these practices that bring us closer to more constantly nurturing and integrating values as the life-inspiring yeast in how we live, relate, work and lead in co-existence with others.

For the next step in your journey with reflection, I invite you to take your "red zone" story, the one that you decided not to act one, through the GVV Canvas process. Put your story at the centre of the canvas and use the questions in each of the elements to reflect on it.

If you wish, you could also take the other story, the one in which you did act on your values, through the same process and think of how you could perhaps have handled it differently with the insight that you now have.

Now reflect on the following questions:

- What new insights are you gaining about the potential of resolving values conflicts successfully?
- With what you have learned, how might you approach a values conflict differently from now on?
- How do you foresee using the GVV Canvas in values conflicts you may be challenged by in future?

CHAPTER 5

NURTURING PERSONAL VALUES CONSCIOUSNESS

> There are things we can do to make it more likely that we will voice our values and that we will do so effectively: namely, reflection, practice and coaching.
>
> —*Mary Gentile*

INTRODUCTION

Values are real. However, they need you and me to be made real in who we are, in what we say and do, and how we relate, communicate and act. Without you and me, values are only concepts; with and among you and me they shape the quality of life, relationships and work we are capable of. If values need us to be real, it means that we must accept agency for making them real. If we want to better navigate through the "red zones" of values conflicts and consciously create more "yellow zone" experiences, there is work to be done.

What does this work refer to? Simply put –

> **we must cultivate the consciousness that will enable us to respond more confidently and competently to values conflicts when they occur as well as build a proactive and sustained values-driven orientation.**

As we previously said, values should not only matter amid conflict; they always matter and must be consciously nurtured over time. This nurturing is about honing our personal moral consciousness and exercising values-driven responsiveness in our spheres of responsibility and influence. This is as much a personal responsibility as it is done in relation with others.

Nurturing values consciousness is about sensing or knowing when we are confronted with a values conflict and being in touch with how we think, feel and may or may not want to act in response to it. Through nurturing this consciousness, we enhance our capacity for taking ownership, showing courage, acting on, and communicating about what we believe is right. Building our capacity for moral consciousness, confidence and competence is not only beneficial for values-driven responsiveness in the present, but it also builds proactive capabilities for the future.

While nurturing our values-driven consciousness is a personal imperative, we need to remind ourselves that values are at the same time interpersonally shared. By nurturing our capacity for values-driven action we are not only building our own moral agency; we are also honouring the moral principles and aspirations of others we are in relationship with or have a responsibility towards. In making values work there is a virtuous feedback loop: we nurture what we have inherited, and we help build and expand what will be in the interest of the common good. I can subscribe to Rubin and Riggio's[34] view that "the decision regarding ethics must be made within individuals before it can be made between individuals", as long as we see this as a reciprocal process. With this I mean that today I might be the one exercising the initiative for values-driven action while tomorrow I might be the one at the centre of someone else's values conflict. As values-driven people we must aspire to maintain integrity and consistency but also remain conscious of our own imperfections and vulnerability and being open to be corrected.

In this chapter, we focus on mastering helpful practices through which we can strengthen our capacity for values consciousness and responsiveness. Staying with the process orientation of the book, I will focus on those practices that I use in teaching and training interventions. These include reflective practices, building responsible leadership competencies and mutual learning exercises. We learn and grow these practices like a baker, by activating the yeast of values and following its interactions with different combinations of ingredients and in different settings of application.

Reflective practices

In a programme on ethical leadership that I have been presenting over the last five years, I require from participants to write a short story about an ethical challenge they have personal knowledge or experience of. The challenge should preferably be about an issue at work, one in which ethical values are being compromised resulting in damage to individuals, important relationships, the organisation or external stakeholders. In the instructions, I request them to write the story as if it is a newspaper article in which they introduce the situation, the protagonist (which could be themselves or another person) and the other role-players involved. Regarding the main character, I prompt them to consider the protagonist's feelings about the situation, the values that seem to be at stake for the protagonist, and the consequences of acting vs not acting. Lastly, I encourage them to frame the burning question that the protagonist seems to be confronted with. I furthermore instruct them to use pseudonyms instead of real names to protect the identity of the people implied in the situation.

Over the years of doing this, I have gathered a sizeable collection of stories and gained much insight into the values conflicts that people face in the workplace. I can summarise these conflicts in three broad categories:

- Values conflicts involving *people*, for example, in performance management practices, absenteeism, the abuse of sick leave, sexual harassment, romantic relationships at work, recruitment without due process, dubious career advancement practices, remuneration issues, workplace cultures, breach of confidentiality, and the abuse of travel claims.
- Values conflicts involving *money* and financial management, for example, fraud, bribery, and/or corruption regarding procurement, investments, donations, conflict of interest, tax compliance, transfer pricing, manipulation of financial results, and redemption procedures.
- Values conflicts related to *power* abuse abound and, apart from including accounts of both categories mentioned above, point to board-level or political interference, especially in the areas of finance, staff appointments and procurement practices.

These stories have benefit for both me and the participants. From my perspective, the stories prepare me for knowing what participants in the programme are struggling with. In this way, every programme cohort represents a microcosm of situations at work that put their capacity for values-driven behaviour under pressure. One cannot but pity the fact that many people – leaders and managers in the case of this programme – are working under such conditions in so many organisations, whether in business, government, academia or civil society. From a participant's perspective, writing such a story offers an opportunity for individual self-reflection in relation to the contexts in which they live, relate, work and lead. The stories they write are mostly remarkably personal and one can sense the authors' hunger and thirst for insight, encouragement and empowerment.

These stories are therefore more than mere training tools. They become avenues for reflection about the self as a moral agent in ethically adverse environments. This begs the question about the role that reflection can play in making moral sense of such surroundings and turning them into learning sites for more confident and competent responsiveness in the future.

De Déa Roglio and Light[35] refer to reflective practice as "the ability to make sense of uncertain, unique, or conflicted situations of professional practice – and is based on the concepts of knowing-in-action, reflection-in-action and reflection-on-action". Knowing-in-action, they describe as spontaneous and part of our daily activities as we go about operations, observations and decisions. It is almost like doing without conscious thinking. However, should we be unusually surprised by experiences that do not fit this mode of knowing-in-action, we may either brush it aside or respond to it through conscious reflection. At this point, De Déa Roglio and Light[36] follow Schön's[37] work on the reflective practitioner, more specifically his distinction between reflecting-in-action and reflection-on-action. Reflecting-in-action is about reshaping what is being done while doing it, for example, by changing strategies or reframing problems on the proverbial spot. Reflecting-on-action is about thinking back after action, or pausing in action in order to reflect on how knowing-in-action may have produced an unexpected outcome.

Reflecting on the stories of programme participants in the ethical leadership programme, one can sense how their *knowing-in-action* was no longer working for them. The confrontation with a values conflict that is simultaneously contrary to what they believe is right and goes against established organisational protocols, prompts reason for reflection for them. Reading through their stories one can observe how their *reflection-in-action* is playing out. The underlying questions in these stories are, "What is going on?" and "What am I going to do about it?" The classroom experience that follows thereafter, introduces them to *reflection-on-action*. This happens when they get introduced to the frameworks, methods and tools under discussion in this book, for example, the Tale of Two Stories exercise or the use of the Giving Voice to Values Canvas. Both instruments can help with strengthening reflective practices and thereby build capacity for values-driven responsiveness. We will reflect on the use of the Tale of Two Stories exercise now and return to the Giving Voice to Values Canvas later.

Let's return to your personal Tale of Two Stories again. This exercise, when used in hindsight, helped you to revisit two values conflict experiences, one in which you acted and the other in which you decided not to act to address the conflict. Let's revisit your stories now by following a reflective pathway as set out below:

- *Knowing-in-action:* What, in both your stories, made you realise that you were faced with something that does not fit your expectations, particularly your values, so that you could not act as if everything is normal? What in it made you pause from continuing with your normal practice? Now, if you transfer these insights to other values conflicts that you experience from time to time, what patterns do you become aware of, both in terms of the context(s) in which such conflicts happen and your responses toward them?
- *Reflecting-in-action:* The Tale of Two Stories contains questions about the presence of other role players, what motivated you to speak up or not, what you said or did or not, what the outcomes were, and what would have made it easier for you to act on your values. Now, from a reflecting-in-action perspective, we know that a values conflict comes with emotional triggers, with weighing the consequences of speaking up versus shutting up, and of battling with rationalisations. How can these insights help you to better understand your default

responses amid values conflicts? How can it help you pause, analyse what you are being challenged with and take ownership for how you might choose to respond?

- *Reflecting-on-action:* The Tale of Two Stories is also an exercise in self-discovery. Beyond the detail and the comparison between the two stories and the motivations for acting vs not acting on your values, it tells you something about lessons you have learned and strengths and weaknesses in yourself that you have discovered that you can transfer to similar future experiences. We often refer to "hindsight as a perfect science", but insight from hindsight can be turned into positive value for future reference. Gentile[38] refers to the importance of being yourself and developing your own voice.[39] By reflecting-on-action, what have you discovered about yourself that may shape your style and strengthen your competence and courage for future values conflicts?

Journalling, if not just done descriptively, but reflectively, helps us to develop critical insights about ourselves in relation to our being, our experiences and our relationships, all of which are essential for the development of our values consciousness, confidence and competence.

Having highlighted the value of the Tale of Two Stories for reflection about and amid values conflicts, I also want to raise a warning, namely, that the practice of reflection should not be limited to experiences of trouble. Regular reflection can be done in a variety of ways, some more structured and others more spontaneous. Reflection can happen through keeping a personal journal, doing mindfulness exercises, and pursuing creative interests. While people have different preferences for practicing reflection, the value of regular journalling lies in the continuity that it brings to one's reflections. Journalling helps with learning from experiences as well as connecting the dots between experiences over time. Journalling is a practice and process that keeps the metaphorical baker in us awake. Through journalling we may enter into conscious reflection on how authentic and effective we are in adding the yeast of values to our daily interactions with others.

If you are already in the habit of mindful reflections, and journalling in particular, I encourage you to include your values-based experiences into it as well. If you have not tried journalling yet, I encourage you to do so. You only need two things to start, namely, a book or an app and time that you regularly set aside for it. Timewise, I recommend that you do it once a week. If you prefer an electronic app over a book, consider something such as Microsoft OneNote, Day One or Penzu. Whether you are already used to reflection, or making a start with it, the threefold pattern that I discussed above provides a helpful framework for ordering your thoughts: knowing-in-action, reflecting-in-action and reflecting-on-action. For reflecting you can work on a values conflict of the past or on one that you are in the midst of and preparing your response for.

Responsible leadership competencies

You may have noticed the recent emphasis on responsible leadership in literature. If you did, you probably wondered whether this is yet another theory of leadership added to the vast array of existing ones: autocratic leadership, charismatic leadership, servant leadership, and ethical leadership, to name a few. It may feel like more than enough to become confused about. This is not the place to get into a theoretical discussion and comparison of leadership theories, but there is a reason why I want to highlight responsible leadership as such. While we may expect all leaders to be responsible, responsible leadership as concept speaks to something different. According to Maak and Pless[40], responsible leadership can be understood as "a social-relational and ethical phenomenon which occurs in social processes of interaction". In a more elaborate definition, they refer to responsible leaders as having –

> the intellectual capacity to cognitively seize, process and assess complex situations, problems and developments from different stakeholder viewpoints and with respect to diverse and sometimes conflicting objectives; who act according to a humane and moral values base, show authenticity and integrity, and care for the needs and interests of others, thereby demonstrating good character; who use relational intelligence (RI) in interacting with stakeholders and apply emotional and ethical intelligence in coping with emerging conflicts of interests, while making far-reaching decisions and reconciling ethical dilemmas.[41]

Say no more! The above quotation corresponds well with the propositions that we have thus far developed about values, their meaning and significance and the importance of making them real in the relationally embedded contexts within which we operate.

Since the publication of Maak and Pless's seminal article in 2006, they and other scholars did much to further develop responsible leadership in concept and theory and promote its application in different contexts. One such development is the Competency Assessment of Responsible Leadership[42], commonly referred to as CARL. I often use CARL as a framework for reflection on ethical action in practice and include it in some versions of values workshops and related programmes.

CARL consist of five competency dimensions, namely stakeholder relations, ethics and values, self-awareness, systems understanding and change and innovation. These competencies are juxtaposed in a matrix relationship with the modalities of knowledge, skills and attitude. Once participants completed the assessment and received their personalised feedback, I do two exercises with them. The first is a short individual essay in which they reflect on the feedback they received and the second is a team-based problem-solving exercise in which they apply the competency framework to a case in practice that presents one or other moral problem to resolve. In table 5.1 below, the first and second columns respectively contain the five competencies and their definitions as available on the CARL2030 website. The third and fourth columns contain the questions that I use for individual reflections and team-based problem solving, respectively. The problem-solving approach can also be used individually. In the reflection section at the end of the chapter, you will find information about how you also can do the assessment online and receive your personalised feedback report.

Table 5.1: Applications of the Competency Assessment of Responsible Leadership

Competencies	**Definitions**	**Questions for individual reflection**	**Questions for problem-solving**
Stakeholder relations	Identifying and integrating stakeholder groups. Dealing with conflicting interests and find consensus. Appreciating the positive in diversity.	Who are the most important stakeholders in your life and career? Why do they matter? Are there any that you may want to improve your relationship with?	Who are the stakeholders in the situation? What impacts, effects or interests are involved?
Ethics and values	Knowing your values and what's right and wrong. Acting according to ethics and values. Being honest, fair, and responsible.	What values matter to you most? In what areas do you feel challenged? What rationalisations may keep you from speaking/acting?	What issues regarding values and ethics emerge from the situation? Why do these issues exist?
Self-awareness	Knowing yourself and understanding the importance of reflection. Learning from mistakes. Sharing your developmental challenges.	How do you develop your awareness about yourself in relationships? What feedback do you solicit or get and how to you respond to it?	What feelings and thoughts are prompted for us in this situation? What moves us towards engagement with it?

Competencies	Definitions	Questions for individual reflection	Questions for problem-solving
Systems understanding	Understanding systems and their inter-dependencies. Seeing the big picture. Working across boundaries. Defending long term perspectives.	How are the different areas of your life interconnected? How do you consider the short- and long-term impact of what you say, decide or do? What areas might be in need of attention and reconnection?	What interdependencies are present in the situation and how might they inform the possibilities and limitations for problem-solving? What will the consequences be of action vs inaction?
Change and innovation	Understanding the drivers and enablers of innovation. Acting to bring about change. Being open, curious, courageous and adaptable.	What are the changes you intend to work on, for example, in terms of yourself, your personal or work relationships, your team or organisation, or even your role in society? How will you know that you are making progress?	What possibilities might exist to bring this situation to a solution in the best interest of all stakeholders involved?

How is this assessment and the exercises that I base on it relevant for nurturing values-driven consciousness? Two sets of observations apply. In the case of the individual reflection exercise, it is interesting to note how participants firstly try to come to terms with the scores they received on each of the competencies and the assessment as a whole. Thereafter a different process sets in as they reflect to make meaning of the feedback they received on each of the competencies. Over time I have noticed interesting patterns in these individual reflections as described below.

Regarding *stakeholder relations*, participants frequently point toward developing a different awareness of the relational embeddedness of their lives, whether in domestic or work-related terms. It is not uncommon to read about a renewed appreciation for positive relationships (mostly family and friends) and the acknowledgement of challenging ones (mostly related to work, for example, managers). Regarding *self-awareness*, I find it interesting how positive participants can be become about their self-awareness and commitment to grow and develop toward what many describe as their "way toward full maturity". Regarding *systems understanding*, participants generally show an openness to accept that they may not always attend to the big picture or take a wide or long enough perspective on interdependent matters in situations of decision-making. And in relation to *change and innovation*, it is quite often the case that participants regard themselves as more change-friendly and adaptable than what was reported by the assessment. They seem nevertheless quite eager to learn and develop in this regard, especially for the benefits that it might hold for their working environments.

You may have noticed that I left reflections on *ethics and values* out of the sequence in which the competencies appear in the CARL framework. I deliberately did so, because in this case there is a pattern that requires a more elaborate discussion. On *ethics and values*, many participants are often unpleasantly surprised by the outcomes of the assessment. While thinking about themselves as truly ethical people who are committed to always doing the right thing, many do not take it lightly when their CARL feedback points toward gaps and indicate some work for them to be done in this area. In none of the other competencies does the assessment touch a sensitive nerve as is the case with ethics and values. Many participants will go as far as questioning the validity of the assessment instrument. When I then discuss it with them, their resistance softens as they begin to understand the gap that might exist between their espoused position and the way they respond - or may be reluctant to respond - to matters of values and ethics in practice. The latter becomes especially tangible in power relationships where they often experience pressure to do things that go against their values as well as in demanding and competitive environments where efficiency considerations tend to overpower moral concerns.

While it might not have been the intention of the CARL developers to prioritise values and ethics above the other competencies, I largely regard it as the glue of the whole framework. Values and ethics are core to the quality and experience of (stakeholder) relations, core to our self-awareness, the driving force in our decisions and actions, and essential for what we might regard as responsible and sustainable change and innovation for the common good.

Regarding the CARL-based problem-solving exercise (the fourth column in the table) you may have noticed that there is a different angle to the questions. I frequently observe the propensity of especially businesspeople to approach problems with quick answers based on utility and efficiency. Using the CARL-framework helps to slow the process down and start with a proper understanding of the stakeholder landscape within which a problem is situated. Stakeholders are real people, whether they present as individuals or groups. Apart from the values that might be at stake for stakeholders, there is also the question about whether or not they will be treated in a values-driven manner, meaning that they experience respect, fairness and understanding in how they are interacted with. When participants follow the questions, working from a stakeholder analysis to the values and ethics at stake, and bringing their own selves into the discussion, they develop a more holistic understanding of the problem, and they increase the range of options available for effective and ethical problem-solving. What literally happens in following this method is to move people with a propensity for relying on their knowing-in-action to a place of reflecting in and on action. Knowing-in-action has its place and often comes with deep experience, but it also carries the risk of applying quick and narrow solutions to systemic

Where stakeholders experience displeasure about something, it implies that they have been impacted in a way that created a values conflict for them. From a values and ethics perspective that impact – and their response to it – is a signal not to be ignored.

challenges. Reflecting in and on action slows the process down and improves the prospects for more holistic solutions as portrayed in the story below.

In a workshop, I observed a group of financial managers applying the CARL framework to a problem-solving scenario. I arranged a roleplay-based case study in which six working groups had to consider an application from a smally dairy farmer who approached their bank for a loan to establish a solar plant on his farm. The initial reaction from most working groups was to deem the application unacceptable. However, as they engaged with the sequence of questions proposed in the CARL problem-solving framework, all the groups started seeing new possibilities and arrived at the conclusion that a loan, tied to certain terms and conditions, can be granted. In the end we had six different proposals from which all could learn. The reflective thinking process reconnected them to a values-driven decision-making approach through which their initial financially restricted judgement could be transformed into an implementable solution with benefits for multiple stakeholders.

How does CARL help us with making values real? When used reflectively, CARL helps us to better understand the important role that values play in stakeholder relations, how we listen to and understand the needs and interests of others from a values-driven perspective and how values might inform how we respond through the decisions and actions that we take. In CARL we have another framework to use in our baker's arsenal as it offers a methodical pathway for working the yeast of values into the dough of problem-solving.

Participants in CARL receive a personalised feedback report speaking to the competencies they may need to pay special attention to. The feedback contains recommendations for development combined with links to articles and videos they might find insightful. In the reflection section at the end of the chapter you will find the instructions for how to complete your own CARL assessment and receive a feedback report.

Learning together

We hold values individually and we share them relationally. Making values real is as much a personal task as it is a shared responsibility. If we accept this premise, it follows that conversations will play a key role in nurturing our values-driven consciousness, confidence and competence. As we share and listen in our communicative interactions, we reciprocally become sounding boards for one another, and we mutually encourage one another for values-driven practice. We learn and grow together.

In this section I discuss three ways of learning together that enhance our capacity for making values real. These practices are values conversations, active listening, and peer coaching.

Values conversations

In chapter 2, I described a method through which we can explore the meaning and significance of values. As a reminder the method is based on three questions: What does a specific value mean for us in practice? What do we gain from practicing this value? What results from neglecting or violating this value? This simple conversational exercise helps people to make the meaning of values their own and bring the realisation thereof within their reach. In this section, I'd like to go further and discuss the developmental power of values conversations.

A few years ago, I did a study on the work of Jurgen Habermas, one of the most influential philosophers of our time. Habermas became especially known for his Theory of Communicative Action. Habermas distinguishes three types of action in human interactions, namely instrumental, strategic and communicative.[43] The descriptions below explain how they differ in their nature and intended outcomes:

- An action is *instrumental* when it is executed by means of technical rules and assessed in terms of the efficiency of outcomes. We may recognise instrumental action, for example, in general information sharing, standard operating procedures, monitoring and evaluation or reporting activities.
- An action is *strategic* when it is based on rational choice and intended to influence the decisions of others, often in an egocentric, prescriptive and authoritarian manner. We will observe this, for example, where people in positions of power dictate vision and strategy without wider consultation or expect adherence to their decisions and instructions based on their rank and title in an organisation.

- In *communicative* action, "participants are not primarily oriented to their own individual successes; they pursue their individual goals under the condition they can harmonise their plans of action on the basis of common situation definitions". Evidence of communicative action, for example in an organisation, will be found in inclusive consultations and dialogue with internal and external stakeholders, collaborative problem-solving processes, and decision-making that incorporates the views and interests of all concerned.

This theory holds relevance for our discussion on making values real, especially when it comes to the quality of our conversations. For now, we are interested in the important implications that communicative action has for the quality of values conversations that we'd like to enjoy in our interpersonal and work-related interactions. Its distinction of and relation to strategic and instrumental action will be revisited again later in the book.

Every participant can question anything, introduce new ideas and topics as they see fit, and accept the possibility that their own opinions might be challenged, even to the point of being willing to change.

Another Habermasian concept that is important for our discussion of values conversations is the notion of the "ideal speech situation". Its connection with communicative action is almost self-evident. While we can refer to a variety of communicative human interactions as speech situations, the ideal one is a conversation where there is no power imbalance between participants and where they can reach an understanding on the basis of consensus. This does not mean that there will be no debate about a topic under discussion, but the manner in which a mutually agreed outcome is achieved has an inherent participatory quality to it. Edgar[44], an interpreter of Habermas' work, refers to this kind of communication as situations in which participants presuppose each other's sincerity and truthfulness and accepts each other's competence to participate.

More will be said about Habermas' theory of communicative action in the next chapter. For now, the above is enough to relate it to the process-based approach that I propose for values work, especially in workshops. Every workshop must be thoroughly entrenched in a communicative action approach. We do not set up values conversations to serve the intentions of instrumental efficiency or a strategic action orientation whereby people are just spoken to, prescribed and taught about values. No, we set conversations up as communicative opportunities for mutual exploration and consensual agreement about what values – even organisational ones – mean for them in practice, what they gain from upholding their values and what they lose from compromising or violating them. Furthermore, every workshop provides a series of conversations (in other words, speech situations) in which participants are enabled to listen to and learn from one another as well as come to agreements on how they can turn their values into action. Thirdly, I want to mention the egalitarian and democratic spirit of values workshops. Pre-existing power relationships are relativised by ensuring that participants of all ranks form part of and are being valued and heard throughout the conversation.

For nurturing values-driven consciousness through conversations we need a communicative context in which participants, despite their differences in rank and responsibility, for example, managers and employees, can engage and build consensus freely and as equals. To emphasise this point, I cannot phrase it better than Habermas[45] himself:

> Members of our species become individuals in and through being socialised into networks of reciprocal social relations, so that personal identity is from the start interwoven with relations of mutual recognition. This interdependence brings with it a reciprocal vulnerability that calls for guarantees of mutual consideration to preserve both the integrity of individuals and the web of interpersonal relations in which they form and maintain their identities.

From experience we know the loneliness that may accompany values uncertainty or conflicts and the difference it makes when the burden is shared, and we can speak or act on the strength of collective wisdom.

While values are precious to us as individuals, we learn and experience their meaning in relationships. Reflective practices, as discussed before, strengthen our personal values awareness and responsiveness. Conversations of the communicative action type enable conceptual clarification, shared meaning and support for making values real in practice. Herein lies the empowering potential of what Habermas refers to as "reciprocal vulnerability".

Active listening

Recall a conversation in which you felt not really listened to or understood, or received advice or instructions that you have not asked for. The person you wanted to interact with was either too preoccupied with other things to take you seriously, too insensitive to your concerns to listen attentively, or too absorbed in their own beliefs to be interested in a real conversation. These situations often play out at home, at school or in organisations in situations where people with authority, such as parents, teachers or managers, either do not make time to really listen or overpower conversations with a one-directional intent. To say it in Habermasian terms, you were looking for a communicative speech situation and got a strategic or instrumental response instead.

Granted, many speech situations in life are simply occasions in which we share information, obtain instructions for how something should be done, or agree on matters of operational or procedural relevance and can be dealt with quite speedily. However,

> **in matters where moral sensitivity is required and values conflicts might be at stake, there is reason to make room for a different mode of communicative engagement.**

Tanzanians taught me the Swahili concept of "pole, pole" which means "slowly, slowly". In matters of ethical concern "pole, pole" is a call to mindfulness and an appeal to slow a certain speech situation down, for example, a critical conversation, important decision or operational process, so that a values-driven outcome can be deliberated about. Active listening is a process and skill that can assist this ideal.

What is active listening? Spataro and Bloch[46] describes it as a communication skill that brings about a connection between a listener and a speaker in which "the listener gives the speaker full attention via inquiry, reflection, respect and empathy". In this interaction, the listener's goal is twofold, namely, to listen with dedicated interest and to develop a proper understanding of what the speaker communicates. Apart from being fully attentive to the speaker, the listener suspends any form of judgment and refrains from advice. Questions are allowed in as far as further elaboration by the speaker will benefit better understanding.

How is active listening related to the nurturing of values-driven consciousness? I use active listening as an essential building block of every values workshop. Right at the beginning, participants do not introduce themselves but are introduced by someone else after a conversational engagement. The process starts with an exercise in which participants choose a conversation partner whom they potentially are the least familiar with. In these dyads they then have a conversation around getting to know one another better and establishing what they would like to learn in the workshop. Afterwards they introduce one another to others, whether in plenary or in a small group. You may ask what is so values-related about this notion of getting to know and speaking on behalf of someone else. Although the exercise is a fun way to do mutual introductions, its real meaning lies in the establishment of a relationship and the enactment of at least two values, namely, respect in the sense of attentive listening and compassion in the sense of understanding the other person in context. Lastly, this exercise also establishes a foundation for trust among participants as they entrust personal information, opinions and questions to someone to present on their behalf. What often surprises me is how little people who have been working together in the same organisation or department know one another in more personal terms, how precious they find the opportunity for showing interest in someone else, and how seriously they take the task of truthfully and sincerely introduce one another. This says a lot about the undervaluing of the human factor in organisations.

A second opportunity for active listening comes with the Tale of Two Stories exercise. If we follow Habermas, this exercise is about comparing two speech situations, the one being a values conflict in which the person spoke up and acted and the other in which they did not. After participants have done their individual written reflections on the two situations, I ask them to form pairs for an active listening exercise in which they interview and represent each other in plenary feedback. They enter this exercise with the following instructions in mind: to listen respectfully, to suspend judgement, to refrain from advice, to only ask questions for clarification if necessary, to treat what they have heard with the necessary confidentiality, and to divide their available time equally. Back in plenary they are requested to share what they have learned about acting vs not acting on values from listening to each other. These conversations, and the feedback, thereafter, are characterised by a recognition of mutual vulnerability - even consolation - that all of us, at some point in our lives, have gone through values conflicts and have stories of success or failure to share. Active listening creates a speech situation in which these stories can be shared and learned from in a non-judgmental context.

A last example of active listening I want to share, comes from the use of the appreciative inquiry approach.[47] Appreciative inquiry, in short, represents an approach to change which is not deficit-based and premised on root cause analysis and gap-closing strategies. It relies on the discovery of potential and learning from previous positive experiences. Participants are asked to do an active listening interview in pairs focused on values-driven leadership in practice and based on four questions. The questions are the following:

- Tell me a story about the best experience you have ever had of working with a values-driven leader. What were the circumstances? What do you remember about the person?
- What did this person's leadership inspired and enable you to do or become?
- When practiced at its very best, what is life-giving about values-driven leadership in a team or workplace?
- What dreams do you have for your own development as a values-driven leader in the relationships or teams that you are a part of?

After having mutually interviewed each other in pairs, participants give feedback on behalf of their conversation partners, focusing on those elements which they were most inspired by or learned something valuable from. Whereas active listening in the case of the Tale of Two Stories creates a context for shared vulnerability, the appreciative inquiry interview creates a sense of inspiration, namely that living, relating and leading in a values-driven way is indeed within the reach of every person.

Active listening is simultaneously a communication skill and a lived expression of values in action.

It is about listening to someone else respectfully and with undivided attention and then representing them as truthfully as possible. Furthermore, active listening, relativises power relationships and democratises conversations. I have seen, for example, how active listening resulted into junior people representing the contributions or opinions of senior ones and the other way round. Consequently, voices that are seldom being heard are amplified and those that are mostly heard are somewhat tuned down in conversations.

There is another benefit to active listening that should not be underestimated. I often remind people in positions of authority of the value of active listening as a leadership practice. People who approach you with a burden to discuss, do not necessarily seek answers or instructions; they mostly desire an opportunity for sharing and understanding. Granting them this opportunity is to respect them and create space for their need to be seen and heard. Sending them away without hearing them out does not make the problem go away; instead, the discussion of the problem just goes elsewhere. That "elsewhere" might be places where the problem festers and contaminates perceptions, relationships and culture. That "elsewhere" might ultimately be the press. Cultivating a habit of active listening is therefore also an act of nurturing values-driven consciousness and responsiveness in organisations.

Peer coaching

Peer coaching is a form of learning and developing together with others through, among other things, the sharing of ideas, reflecting on current practices, providing feedback, solving problems, and learning new skills.[48] In a workplace environment this will typically happen among colleagues or people with similar experience levels. In a training environment people with different experience levels may be drawn into peer coaching as a result of similar learning and skills development needs. Peer coaching is an ideal vehicle for enabling people to make values real.

Gentile[49] recommends specifically that peer coaching be used in relation to the practice of rescripting. She goes as far as saying that "insightful and supportive peer feedback on discussants' proposed "scripts" and strategies for responding to values conflicts is an essential part of the Giving Voice to Values approach". She regards it as a problem-solving approach in which speakers (those who share their proposed responses to a values conflict) and listeners (those who act as coaches) work together on building effective responses to values conflicts. She furthermore offers a process-based template for how speakers and listeners can effectively work through and respond to a values conflict, focusing especially on the proposed scripts and action plans. Those in the peer coaching situation who listen will focus on considering the strengths of the approach, the questions that remain unresolved, the impact that the response might have, and improvements to still be considered. Those who speak are encouraged to consider the strengths of their intended approach and to combine it with reflection on the remaining concerns and questions raised by their peers. She furthermore recommends a set of process questions regarding audience, timing, support, information, situation, etc. Such peer coaching engagements lead to the mutual strengthening of the participants' values-driven responsiveness. Both speakers and listeners gain from it.

At this point, I'd like to bring the Giving Voice to Values Canvas back into our discussion. In the previous chapter, I explained how the canvas can be used individually for working through a values conflict. There is personal reflective value in using it. It also fits very well with the two modes of reflection referred to earlier in this chapter, namely reflecting-in-action and reflecting-on-action. As a one-page overview of a values conflict, it helps the user to connect the dots and build a response in an iterative manner. Having said this, the canvas also doubles up very well as a peer coaching framework. I use it in some values workshops by asking participants to consider a values conflict for which they want to develop a response and action plan. I then invite them to use the canvas, and the questions that accompany it, to plot out the whole narrative, combined with their response and action plan for presentation to their peer group. In the peer coaching session that follows, each will get an opportunity to present in an atmosphere of active listening followed by a discussion of the type that Gentile recommends, namely for the listeners to ask questions, highlight the strengths and consider improvements before implementation. Workshop participants normally feel that this peer coaching exercise, based on the canvas, helps them to get a grip on what they experience and how they might go about addressing it in practice. From my observations participants appreciate the opportunity to share their values conflict narratives in a trustful environment with people who listen to them with undivided attention. The discussions are intense, and the aftermath exudes a sense of relief and gratitude.

Peer coaching goes beyond adding the yeast of values to the dough of conversations; it is more like breaking bread together as we feed one another's capacity for making values real in practice.

CS Lewis somewhere wrote that "we read to know we are not alone". A values conflict can be a lonely place until shared in a trusted environment of understanding, feedback, encouragement and support. Peer coaching alleviates this sense of loneliness. And where peer coaching happens in a context where people work together, there remains a sense of mutual interest and accountability in the aftermath of it. In this way, we build surplus capacity for values-driven consciousness and competence in practice.

Conclusion

We think of values as the aspirational beliefs that we hold about human behaviours, expressing how we prefer or agree to live and relate, and determining what we regard as right or wrong in particular situations and the decisions we make as a result. In this chapter, we focused on practices that may grow our capacity for making this understanding of values real. Some of these practices lean more towards individual and reflective mindfulness while others are essentially interpersonal and conversational. Together these different types form a reciprocal loop with mutual benefit for the individually reflective and mutually conversational processes of building values-driven consciousness and competence. What essentially happens in the process is that we improve our capacity for moral imagination, which means that we learn how to look beyond the constrictions of a values conflict and identify possibilities for resolving it constructively and ethically.

What is moral imagination? Biss[50] defines it as "the capacity to generate possibilities for good action in response to well-perceived moral circumstances" She makes the point that stories often represent accounts of moral imagination that theories are less able to explain. Through a story, you just know when a particular response to a moral problem has beaten the odds. Lederach[51] defines it as "the capacity to imagine something rooted in the challenges of the real world yet capable of giving birth to that which does not yet exist". As a specialist in peacebuilding, Lederach refers to four essential disciplines at the heart of moral imagination, which, to my mind, are suitably applicable to values work. These disciplines are the centrality of relationships, the refusal to fall prey to either-or thinking, providing space for creativity, and the willingness to risk. Werhane[52] refers to three types of moral imagination: reproductive (awareness of context and scripts), productive (new possibilities within a situation or role) and creative (envisioning new possibilities including self and others).

Instead of operating in the limiting confinement of "what should be done", a focus on "what could be done" makes a different kind of moral reflection and values conversation possible.

All of these accounts of what moral imagination means, connect well with the question at the heart of Gentile's GVV approach, namely, "What if you were going to act on your values—what would you say and do?".[53] There is a morally imaginative intent in this question. In this sense, this chapter was about exploring and mastering practices through which we can build morally imaginative capacity for values-driven "what could be done" conversations.

Having now dealt with nurturing personal values consciousness our focus will now shift to whether we can also nurture the moral imagination of an organisation.

For personal reflection purposes I want to encourage you to do the Competency Assessment of Responsible Leadership. The steps are as follows:

- Go to: https://carl2030.org/ and read the overview.
- Go to https://carl2030.org/for-you/ and study the instructions.
- Click on "Take the Test", complete it and submit it together with your email address.
- Receive your report and reflect on the results and recommendations for development.

Once you have done the above, go to table 5.1 and make time to reflect on the questions for individual reflection in the third column. What are you learning from these reflections? What challenges and choices could you do more work on developing your personal values-driven consciousness and competence?

You can also go one step further with CARL and use the problem-solving framework in the last column of table 5.1 to reflect on a personal or work-related challenge of a moral nature. Apply those questions to the situation and see how it stimulates your moral imagination and capacity for values-driven problem solving.

If you are leading a team, you can even introduce the CARL assessment to them. With them having done the exercise, you can discuss the meaning of the competencies for team purposes and use it as a framework for values-driven problem solving. I have worked with leaders who have done this with great success.

CHAPTER 6

INTEGRATING VALUES IN ORGANISATIONS

> We can, however, figure out how to bring our values to life, how to infuse our companies and our business lives with what we stand for, and how to do values better. In short, we can bridge the values gap.
>
> —*Freeman & Auster*

INTRODUCTION

I once did a session on "values integration in personal and organisational practice" with a group of MBA students from different countries and industries. Most of them were practicing managers representing different levels of seniority in their organisations. As in most values workshops, I started the session with a happy - angry exercise followed by an exploration of the meaning and application of the values of honesty, respect, responsibility, fairness and compassion. Upon me wanting to shift the conversation from the personal domain to the workplace, one student almost protested, arguing that it is impossible to apply these values in a business and organisational context. These values, he said, are good for personal and relational benefit, but not suitable for the profit-driven and competitive nature of business and the complexities inherent to organisational life. It was as if several other students in the group felt almost relieved that one amongst them was outspoken enough to voice that which was for them a common experience too. Mixing values into the already complex ingredients of business and organisation was for them a bridge too far. This conversation raised a question that remained ever-present for me: If values are so integral in who we are and how we relate, why is it so challenging to make them real in matters of organisation and business?

Are you part of an organisation? If so, what role do values play in it? If the organisation has a set of values, how is it communicated? How widely is it accepted? How consistently are the values practiced? To what extent do you experience yourself to be playing an active role in making these values real?

Whether we create or join an organisation, whether the organisation is small or large, whether we lead or are being led, our worldviews, our cultural backgrounds, our values, our expertise and our role expectations meet up with others in the same space.

Being part of an organisation involves participating in a complex entity consisting of people with their own unique identities, stories, interests and hopes. One part of getting this dynamism aligned and moving in the same direction is about clarity of purpose, structural support, operational efficiency and role-specific performance. The other part is about getting along and collaborating with others to develop solutions, solve problems, make decisions and deal with conflicts. Values, at least in the understanding promoted in this book, are woven into this whole fabric of organisational dynamics. We seem to assume, often inadvertently, that values will guarantee the alignment and bonding that will keep the whole together. This may be why organisational values statements so often contain three types of values, namely strategic, work and ethical values.[54] With these three types of values, we seem to assume that values will simultaneously anchor, align and inject the purpose we pursue, the way we do our work and the moral quality of our decisions, behaviours and actions. Values can do this for us, but it will not happen automatically. There is integration work to be done.

Much has been written about how this organisational values integration ideal can be pursued. Focusing on practice-oriented resources we can refer to Gentile's Giving Voice to Values approach from which we have already richly gained in several parts of this book. Another commendable work is that of Freeman and Auster[55] on bridging what they call "the values gap" in organisations, specifically through their Values Through Conversations approach. In their book on business ethics, Rossouw and Van Vuuren[56] commit a whole chapter to "ethics and human potential" in organisations. The Ethics Institute, an organisation committed to building an ethically responsible society, developed a rich repository of organisational ethics handbooks around a central model of ethics management containing works on ethical leadership, culture and institutionalisation, conflict of interest and whistleblowing. All these handbooks can be accessed for free at https://www.tei.org.za/publications/.

While being deeply influenced and also indebted by the resources referred to above, I want to continue along the process pathway that we have followed since the beginning of the book. Our quest for making values real continues, but now the focus shifts to how it can be done in organisations and, most importantly, how every organisational participant can play a role in making it happen. Especially important in this chapter will be an expansion of our leading metaphor, namely the yeast effect, and a values integration project that illustrates the realisation thereof in practice. The chapter will close with a discussion of leverage points we have available for values integration in organisations.

The values integration challenge

I once did a programme on ethical leadership with the senior management team of a financial services company. The company had an ethics charter containing six values statements referring respectively to integrity, customer-centricity, respect, trust and accountability, diversity and inclusion, and agility and innovation. The charter spelt out what these values mean and how they should apply in all internal and external stakeholder relations. It also stipulated criteria for sound ethical judgement in situations where the values might be in danger of being violated. However, upon analysing the company's annual report in search of values-related references, I identified 249 statements referring to direct and indirect financial value creation and only one statement referring to values as promoted in its ethics charter. This example might be incidental, but it raises several concerns, the first being that of two types of values, namely strategic and ethical ones and the question about which of these will have the upper hand in situations where ethical judgement might be required. The second concern relates to the dominance of financial value creation and the extent to which the organisation attends to values integration across its investments, transactions, operations and relationships. The third concern relates to the organisation's annual report which was devoid of any statement regarding values integration or how it has dealt with any ethical issues emerging from its operational processes and stakeholder relationships.

From this story, and the one at the beginning of the chapter, we seem to have at least three challenges with making values real in organisations. The first is that the values might be espoused but lack integration with strategic and operational processes. The second is that strategic and operational considerations simply overshadow the personal and relational dimensions of organisational life. The third is that individuals - even managers - might experience the integration challenge as too daunting to consider. Avoiding this integration challenge is not good for any organisation nor for the people who participate in it. If we want to express our humanity and experience meaningful co-existence with others across the different spheres of our lives, and especially at work, this is a task not be avoided. If we accept that this is a bridgeable challenge, the question is how it can be accomplished?

Two sides of the organisational value(s) story

There exists an important interrelationship between two dimensions of an organisation, namely enterprise and community. As an enterprise, an organisation is strategically minded and focused on value creation for stakeholders, whether these are shareholders, customers, or other types of participants and beneficiaries. Value creation, so understood, is measurable and usually refers to financial success in combination with several other criteria, for example, product range, scope of services and market share. As community, an organisation is about people and relationships and how they interact and collaborate internally as well externally with stakeholders. For an organisation, enterprise and community are simultaneously indispensable and inseparable. Enterprise that neglects community will soon run empty of the relational energy it needs for success, and community without an enterprising sense of purpose will be at risk of complacency and mediocrity. For an organisation to be simultaneously successful and reputable it needs to embrace both value creation and values integration. Ideally we want organisations that are both effective and ethical. For a practical and experiential demonstration of this interplay between enterprise and community, I refer you to the "circles in the air" exercise in the appendix on page 148.

Enterprise is about driving the organisation forward through strategy, operations, efficiency, productivity and financial viability. Community is about relationality and pulling together those who participate in the work of the organisation and make it work for its stakeholders.

While the above sounds self-evident, and even ideal in principle, it is easier said than done in practice. More often than not, there is in organisations a tension-ridden relationship between strategic and instrumental action, on the one hand, and communicative action, on the other. Strategic and instrumental action is by nature inclined to focus on control, measurability and efficiency; communicative action is essentially intersubjective, consensus-seeking and norm-producing. Strategic and instrumental actions seek to convince through financial, operational, and technical rationality. While we may prefer strategic, instrumental and communicative action to be reciprocal and mutually informative, the reality is most often that the latter has a hard time to get the attention it deserves in processes of organisational decision making. This may explain why employees, often in jest, refer to their organisations' "values on the wall". Likewise, we notice it when organisations are often in the news for unethical conduct despite their espoused values and codes of ethics. In the case of the latter, closer examination often reveals how the voices of moral reasoning have been suppressed in the expedient pursuit of ethically questionable interests.

More is needed than the mere possession of a set of values, the display thereof in reports and marketing collateral or the inscription thereof in codes and policies. While values are ever-present across the variety of our interpersonal interactions and transactions, they must be consciously evoked, voiced and acted upon to fulfil their purpose.

Organisations have a natural appetite and propensity for strategic and instrumental action. Under this banner, results can more readily be calculated, measured, and factually and graphically presented. Values integration, on the other hand, requires constant dedication to be experienced as authentic and effective. Values integration, therefore, demands that we understand the communicative processes through which values consciousness can be activated, practically applied and constantly nurtured. We also need to understand - and be able to withstand - those forces and factors that undermine and suppress the expression of values in organisational processes.

The irony is that many organisations regard investment in values integration as too time consuming[57] and therefore tend to make it subservient to strategic and operational expediency until an ethical scandal strikes. Thereafter the neglect of values speaks loudly and painfully in the loss of staff morale, public reputation and financial sustainability. The relationship between value creation and values integration must therefore constantly be strengthened. There are too many organisational stories of value creation implosion due to the neglect of values integration to ignore. What can an organisation do to minimise this risk?

Tone from the top and critical mass

There seem to be two popular beliefs regarding progress and success with values integration in organisations. The one is about leadership direction and example and the other is about the scale of member buy-in and commitment. Both beliefs carry merit, and both have shortcomings.

There is merit in the "tone from the top" argument. It is ideal that leaders personify, protect and promote the values that an organisation care about. With a top leader setting the tone and pace and doing so consistently a lot of what values integration is about become easier to accomplish. However, we must also have caution about this argument. If too much is dictated from the top, however praiseworthy it seems to be, values integration may border on enforcement, prescriptive instructions, mass rollout initiatives, compulsory values training, the intolerance of deviance, or the public shaming of anyone stepping out of line. This kind of leadership behaviour is akin to what I have highlighted before, namely strategic rationality: forcing others to accept the leader's view and argument regarding a situation, whether of strategic, operational or moral relevance. This approach does not work well for values integration; it borders on fear induction and limits an organisation's potential to create communicative environments in which authentic values-driven conversations and actions can flourish. Fallout can also pivot in the opposite direction where a top leader fails to set an ethical tone and becomes a barrier for values integration even to the point of being the personification of values conflict rationalisations. Such leaders are often tempted to use their power to protect themselves, to shift the blame onto others, or to ensure the marginalisation or removal of those brave enough to speak up against them. Any of these two scenarios raise the question about the role that other organisation members - those with lesser power - can play in maintaining values-driven agency in their areas of influence and responsibility. Where the leader overpowers, albeit positively intended, it may limit the growth of organisation-wide agency. Where the leader undermines, it may turn an organisation into a moral battlefield.

Turning to the factor of critical mass, we will admittedly desire to be surrounded by a majority of likeminded people who are committed to living the values of the organisation. Few will argue that a critical mass of likeminded people will not make organisational life easier. Just think about the momentum and scale that could be achieved. But here too a warning should be heeded. Is the majority always right? Can values and ethics ever be based on the democratic overweight of numbers? History offers us enough examples where the majority faltered, whether in politics, business or other types of organised environments. So, mass is helpful, but it may also cast shadows. Mass, just like forceful leadership, might also suppress the deviant or marginalised voices that we must listen to, voices that raise internal and external sensitivities that we must know about. Raising values-based criticism in such circumstances may not be welcomed and instead be met by several rationalisations. Critical mass can also pivot in the wrong direction where active support is lent on a wide scale to arguments and causes that cannot be defended on moral grounds. For a values-driven person, this might feel like being permanently in the red zone of values compromises and conflicts.

We may conclude that, positively speaking, the tone from the top and the momentum of critical mass are beneficial, but not necessarily sufficient to represent the full picture of what values integration is all about. Now, let's revisit our baker.

The yeast effect

In the preface to the book, I stated that –

> **values made real, represents the yeast that we need for fulfilling relationships, meaningful work and decisions and actions that advance the ethical best that we are capable of**.

This realisation makes "bakers" of all of us. Throughout the book I left traces, almost like granules of yeast, of what this metaphor may have to do with making values real. The time has come to explore this in more detail.

Credit goes to John Paul Lederach[58] for the metaphor of the yeast. As sociologist and peace builder, he explains how he initially had an interest in how mass and movement can be achieved in processes of social change. He expands on the lures and challenges of the critical mass argument. This argument, he says, is built on the belief that if sufficient attention can be raised and movement initiated by a large enough number of people, there might be a better chance of achieving the social outcomes being sought. While recognising the merit of numbers-based advocacy or protest, Lederach also warns against the potential dark sides thereof. It easily becomes a matter of side-taking and turns society into a social battlefield and dualistic struggle of which numbers become the yardstick of success. Counter-intuitive to its original intentions this approach might turn out to be more destructive and less sustainable over time.

Is there an alternative to critical mass? Lederach proposes one, namely that of "critical yeast". Whereas critical mass originates from nuclear fission and has been translated to the social domain for the sake of understanding the generation of momentum for change at scale and speed, critical yeast has its origin in the baking of bread. Of all the ingredients needed for the baking of bread, the yeast counts amongst the smallest while it is at the same time the indispensable one. Without the yeast being carefully prepared and kneaded into the dough there can be no bread. Nuclear fission occurs when a neutron splits an atom and critical mass for sustained energy release comes from a sufficient number of neutrons keeping on causing the reaction. Yeast, on the other hand, does its work biologically by causing an exponential outcome in coherence with relevant ingredients and interrelated processes. Critical mass originates from pressure, critical yeast from fermentation.

It is not out of the question to think about organisational values integration in terms of critical mass. However, there is a different principle involved in critical yeast. In the case of critical mass, we think in terms of what needs to be done by the greatest among the leaders, supported by the greatest number of participants and through widely scaled activities and mechanisms. In the case critical yeast, we think in terms of who the agents of change might be and their ability to generate over time - and time and time again - the values-driven consciousness and change that an organisation might be in need of.

How can the image of critical yeast help us build pathways for values integration in organisations? The first thing to understand and accept is that the yeast it not about "what" but about "who". The relationship between us as "the bakers" and the yeast as our values is not one of instrumentality, but of embodiment. In the end the yeast is not just about our values, but about us. Over and above *adding* yeast we also *become* yeast in the variety of speech situations in which we have influence, interact with others and connect with them to bring to life the organisational values we have in common. If we accept this principle of also being the yeast by grace of our personal presence and influence, we can start figuring out how this can promote the realisation of values integration in the situations where we relate and operate. A different way of saying the same is that we are capable of having systemic influence and exponential impact through the mediating potential of the values that we bring to action. The story that follows explains the point.

Critical yeast in action

Our quest is about making values real. In this chapter, it is about doing it in organisations. To illustrate how real this may become, I want to share process and practice insights from a values integration project I have been involved with. The project involved six public hospitals and ran over a period of four years, the time of the Covid-19 pandemic included. In chapter 4, I already shared some parts of the story to illustrate how rescripting works. Here I want to share the rollout and impact of the project as a whole. For me, this is sort of a seminal story of which the insights about values integration may have relevance for many other organisations.

The story began in 2018 with Dr Zilla North who was at the time the medical manager of George Hospital in South Africa. She attended a values-driven leadership train-the-trainer workshop co-facilitated by me and Mollie Painter-Morland, professor at Nottingham-Trent Business School. Zilla left the training inspired with the belief that what she learned could have value for George and other hospitals in the same provincial healthcare district. She acquired the necessary permission and funding and got the project underway. Soon she and I co-presented our first Values-driven Leadership for Healthcare Professionals workshop. More workshops followed and we were joined by a third co-facilitator, Prof Louis Jenkins, a medical specialist.

Right at the beginning of the project we had to make four critical decisions. The first was about whether workshop attendance was compulsory or voluntary. We opted for the latter, arguing that values training should never be the proverbial "grudge purchase". Interested participants should attend when they were ready to do so. The second was about the composition of workshop cohorts by means of open invitation or sub-group specific attendance. Should we go for the latter we would keep different disciplines, different hospitals and different layers of authority separate. Eventually we opted for the open mix. The third critical choice was about the duration of workshops. Hospitals are busy places and can barely afford to be short on staff at any point in time. Notwithstanding, we opted for two and a half day workshops presented in retreat conditions with time away from professional and domestic demands. The last choice was about the size of a training cohort. Do we take an unlimited number of participants, or do we cap the attendance? This is the same as asking whether we wanted breadth of participation or depth of engagement. We capped the numbers at twenty participants per workshop.

I share the above, because these choices have important implications for the quality of the learning experience during a values workshop as well as for the organisational values integration that follows afterwards. It may sound like post-facto self-justification, but the choices we made seemed to have been right for the outcomes that we sought. Voluntary participation in smaller and diversely composed cohorts in a retreat environment over a substantial period of time built a dividend of results with long-lasting impacts for the participants, their relationships and their working environments.

If values are nurtured in relationships and if speech situations of the communicative kind are best suited for values conversations and the mastery of skills, then the training environment and facilitation processes should mirror such assumptions.

As a brief intermezzo, I would like to comment on the four sources of values that we worked with in the project, and in the workshops in particular. We used the values of honesty, respect, responsibility, fairness and compassion as a basis for participants to explore the personal and interpersonal value of values. Unpacking these values in terms of what they mean, what we gain by upholding them and loose by violating or neglecting them, provides a shared foundation for what it practically means to give voice to values and sets the scene for more complex conversations to follow. Acknowledging that healthcare is historically speaking a profession rooted in values, we added into the programme a reflection session on the Hippocratic Oath, The Practo Blog for Doctors[59] and the Physician's Pledge of the World Medical Association.[60] These reflections were not done for the sake of debate and argument, but for exploring how the values of a profession and its related services can evolve over time - even centuries - without losing its essential ethos and practice implications. The third layer of values was that of the Western Cape Government, under which auspices the district operates. These values were caring, competence, integrity, accountability, innovation and responsiveness. The last layer was the ethical guidelines of the Health Professional Council of South Africa[61], specifying thirteen values and referring to the healthcare profession as a "moral enterprise". Broadening the scope of our values conversations this wide, was not about jogging anyone's capacity for memory, neither was it to double up on complexity. We believed that the process approach we were promoting, would enable participants to work with and within complementary sets of values as they go about their healthcare activities, whether clinical or administrative, in a wider context.

Over time, we started to notice changes in the workplace that we were very thankful for. Firstly, there was evidence that people were talking differently - more respectfully - to and about one another, especially in high-pressure situations and across the boundaries of different disciplines, functions and organisational layers. As new relationships took shape and established ones became renewed, there emerged a different sense of empathy and understanding for the context of others, especially in view of the diverse backgrounds and communities that people were from. The old silos and hierarchies became penetrable, and the boundaries became softer as interdisciplinary collaboration around difficult issues improved. With healthcare being such a morally contested environment those who attended the workshops attested that they found themselves to be better equipped and confident to have difficult conversations on potentially divisive ethical issues. We also picked up accounts of people who entered the workshops on the verge of burnout but regained their capacity for personal and moral agency and an increased ability to affect change in their professional practices and areas of responsibility.

What happened in the training that made these changes possible? From one perspective we designed the workshops along the lines that I will explain in the next chapter. From another, we simply used the same exercises for giving voice to values that I described in earlier parts of the book. The real answer, I believe, lies at a deeper level and has to do with three factors. The first has got to do with the way in which active listening is built into several of the learning experiences over the duration of the programme. Active listening changes the way in which we express interest in and listen to someone, especially if it is followed by representing that person's story or views in plenary thereafter. Participants often remarked about the responsibility they experience when representing a conversation partner truthfully and authentically in a larger forum.

The second factor has to do with how the conversation pairs for active listening were created, namely that people were invited to choose conversation partners as differently as possible from themselves and as little known to them as possible, even if they have been working in the same organisational setting over time. In doing so we were able cut through the organisational and professional silos and layers and bring people into contact and conversation with others whom they might not have chosen spontaneously. Resulting from this we noticed how people with more organisational authority listened to and presented the stories or views of ones with significantly lesser power and vice versa. Similarly, people with clinical responsibilities listened to and spoke on behalf of those with administrative roles and vice versa. Voices which dominated in the workplace were toned down and those who seldom spoke were now amplified. More examples can be offered, but the point is that these small acts of boundary crossing democratise the conversation environment and contribute to trust building among participants. This newfound mutuality carries over to the workplace where it influences the way organisational participants view and engage with one another.

There is a third factor worth mentioning. At the start of a values workshop we invited participants to consider a values conflict they would like to work on and develop and action plan for during the course of the training experience. At the end, enlightened by the variety of exercises and interpretive lenses, participants present their situation analyses and action plans in an active listening-based peer coaching session to fellow participants. While this is similar to what I discussed in the previous chapter, it is worth mentioning here as well, especially within the context of building capacity for organisational values integration. Earlier I cited examples of new developments and changes we noticed in workplace practices and to my mind many of these can be related to how the learning process supports personal narratives to unfold into transformative values-based organisational benefits. Without naming it as such then, I can now see how critical yeast was activated by people accepting agency for values enactment in one situation after another.

The communicative and supportive setting within which these values-driven action plans are presented and discussed, builds encouragement and confidence for personal agency and organisational values integration. It also fosters mutual accountability for action.

Midway into the project, a research team from the business schools of Stellenbosch and Nottingham-Trent did an impact research study to test the efficacy and sustainability of the training. From the research article resulting from the study, I'd like to highlight its overarching conclusion, namely that of "the mediating potential of relationally embedded values-driven practices to enhance communication, information-sharing, problem-solving and decision-making in workplace settings".[62] It is also this mediating capacity of values that enables organ-

It is this mediating capacity of values and the personal, interpersonal and institutional practices through which they are embodied, embedded and enacted that make organisational values integration a living possibility.

isational actors from different disciplines, functions and responsibility levels to work across boundaries and co-navigate intra-organisational and contextual complexity.

The research, furthermore, highlighted three practices through which shared values generate relational shifts between organisational participants, namely, acknowledging, inviting and leveraging. The practice of acknowledging is about admitting the existence of a values conflict, the emotional discomfort that goes with it and the initiation of the process towards dealing with it. The practice of inviting is about making space and time for relational connections, active listening and entering into values conversations in appropriate situational settings so that values conflicts can be dealt with. Leveraging is the practice of building solutions, changing organisational practices, generating collaboration, addressing issues and making organisational culture change possible.

This story of values integration started small, with one person having a vision of what values-driven leadership can do for healthcare professionals and hospitals in a provincial district. That conviction and the processes that followed thereafter, initiated a values integration process of systemic influence and outcomes. Values have mediating capacity but to make their working real, like yeast, requires time, patience and persistence. Momentum comes where the interplay between the practices of acknowledging, inviting and leveraging are regenerated over and over again, from one communicative speech situation to the next and the next and the next.

Doing it like a baker

Against the background of the healthcare story, what role do you see yourself playing in values integration in the organisation(s) you are a participant in? From the healthcare story I can identify three possible roles for "yeast-based" values integration strategies in organisations. The first role is simply that of personal presence, the second plays out in the functional domain and the third relates to the practice of leadership. Depending on personal circumstances and the type of organisations we take part in we can fulfil more than one, if not all three roles, at the same time. In the discussion that follows, I will focus on these roles in a more business-oriented organisational setting.

The personal role

Similar to yeast, we do not have influence from a position of isolation. Living is about connectedness, interdependence and relationality. Buber[63] says it beautifully: "All actual life is encounter". Values are ingrained into these encounters: if we uphold them, we benefit, if we violate them, we suffer the consequences. While not all interpersonal encounters are driven by moral intent, there is an undeniable moral quality to how we co-exist and collaborate with others.

Making values real in the baker's way suppose that we understand that the mixing of yeast and dough is embedded in multiple processes and relational encounters. A baker's life is inevitably interwoven with that of stakeholders, whether in the kitchen, the shop front or in the community through multiple interactions and transactions. Every encounter is an opportunity for the yeast of values to produce exponential outcomes. The more these encounters produce "yellow zone" outcomes, the better for the baker, the better for the business. Some encounters may turn out to be "red zone" ones and raise values conflicts. If, in the case of the latter, the yeast remains on the shelf, you have made the choice not to speak up and live with the consequences that it might hold over the longer term. In choosing for speaking up and acting on your values, you have dared to put the yeast to work, even if a positive outcome cannot always be guaranteed.

Thinking of the multiple encounters that you may have the opportunity to positively influence in your role as an organisational participant, we have stocked your baking artistry, so to speak, with several methods to be used. Which of them can you take into your ordinary conversational encounters? Which of them do you want to try out in meetings and decisions making processes that you are a participant in? Which of them do you want to use for navigating through the more problematic encounters? Which do you want to sit back with and, through reflection, consider how you can strengthen your values consciousness, confidence and competence?

A baker must know how to relate the chemistry between ingredients with the art of creating a pleasing product. It is a learning process that matures over time as it is done over and over again. A baker captures the results of these learning processes in recipes. In organisations we capture the results of our learning processes in policies and standard procedures. When it comes to values integration, many, if not most, organisations have some sort of ethics architecture, whether as codes of ethics or conduct combined with several policies, that may fulfil this purpose. If you happen to be in an organisation that does have such instruments, do not take them for granted, leave them on the shelf, rather rely on people in other roles than yours to use them, or just consult them in emergencies. Study them and consider how they might support your contribution to organisational values integration. Also study them to know how they might strengthen your values-driven responsiveness. Do this to strengthen your contribution to the positive advancement of values. Do this to know how you might use them in values conflicts to support the rescripting of rationalisations where necessary. They are there for your benefit. Don't allow them to go stale.

At the end of a values workshop, a participant, almost out of the blue, confessed that she may need to rethink the way in which she stands up for her values and beliefs. She has been known as a no-nonsense straight talker who leaves no uncertainty about her opinion on things. However, as consistently values-driven as she is, she often finds herself in destructive spirals of attack-and-defence arguments with win-lose outcomes. "Maybe I should stop turning every difference with others into a fight. Maybe I should change my approach and think differently about how I can better communicate my convictions", she said. She has taken the first step toward embracing the theory of the critical yeast.

The functional role

Values integration applies for every form of organisation, however big or small. In bigger organisations we find role differentiation, even to the point where some end up becoming whole departments. In smaller setups individuals fulfil multiple roles, while in the bigger ones, specialisation of different degrees almost becomes inevitable. These functional roles add another layer to the task of values integration. While it makes our metaphorical bakery more complex, it does not decrease the need for the fermenting capacity of the yeast of values to work throughout the organisation.

Whether you assume multiple functions due to being in a small organisation, whether you are just a participating member in a functional unit within a larger organisation, or whether you have a managerial responsibility, I invite you to consider the values integration possibilities explained below. To make it practical, and where applicable, I'll refer to the five values that we explored the meaning of in chapter 2: honesty, respect, responsibility, fairness and compassion. Depending on your context you may add others as well. Ultimately, the question is how each function, and thereby yourself as an actor, can use the fermenting capacity of values to build the ethical ethos of your organisation.

If you are *a human resource practitioner,* you deal in a very direct sense with the composition and culture of your organisation. What role can you play to ensure a respectful and compassionate workplace where every employee feels valued and engaged? What role can you play to ensure fairness in remuneration? How can you promote diversity, equity and inclusion throughout the organisation? And what about ensuring that values are integrated in recruitment and appointments? What opportunities exist for values integration in training and development?

If in *finance*, you are capable of influencing your organisation's understanding and enactment of resource stewardship. What role can you play in promoting honesty in all transactions? What can you do to instil a responsibility mindset in how people work with the assets of the organisation? What influence can you have on ensuring that goods and services are fairly priced? How may you bring values to bear in conversations on income distribution? To what extent do you consider the cost of the organisation's activities for society and the environment? How do you promote transparency in financial and related reporting to organisational stakeholders and society more broadly?

If you are in the *marketing and sales* domain, you represent the reliability of your organisation's products and services to the wider public. How do you help ensuring that products are safe, and that product information is truthfully presented? How do you contribute to treating customers respectfully and fairly? To what extent do customers and the general public experience understanding, care and compassion when engaging with your organisation?

If you are a specialist in *ethics, legal* and *compliance*, you work at the heartbeat of the organisational ethos. What role can you play in helping organisational participants making positive connections with the organisation's codes and policies? How do you understand the contents, value and use of these instruments? Admittedly these instruments are often regarded as an insurance against ethical risk, but what contribution can you make to bring them to life as an investment in goodness and positive organisational impact for multiple stakeholders?

If your role is of an *operational* or *manufacturing* nature, you work, so to speak in the organisational engine room. How do you ensure that all concerned take pride in their work and collaborate to ensure that standards are followed and that the quality and safety of production outputs can be trusted? How can you help ensure humane conditions where people experience respect, fairness and compassion, even amid the inevitable production pressures they might be working under? What do you do to minimise waste and prevent harm to society and the environment?

If your role is in the *corporate responsibility* and *sustainability* domain, you have a direct involvement in your organisation's impact on the environment, society and economy. How do you help your organisation to develop an integrated sustainability orientation? How can you guide your organisation to treat society and the environment respectfully, responsibly, fairly and with compassion? How do you contribute to truthfulness and accountability in reporting the organisation's environmental, social and economic impact to stakeholders and society in general?

I could refer to several other functional roles as well. The point is that every organisational function is as much about value creation as values integration. In every function you can be the baker at work, building enterprise and community at the same time. Values are the yeast at your disposal to connect and integrate enterprise and community – strategic, instrumental and communicative action – to ensure effective and ethical outcomes.

In addition to your personal presence, a functional role demands a different level of sensitivity for making values real. No function works in isolation. Linkages with other functions must consciously and continuously be made. All functions contribute and need to work together to build an ethical organisation. Not all conversations across functional responsibilities will always be easy and values conflicts and rationalisations are bound to occur. However, the healthcare story tells us that it is possible if we work the yeast of values into the dough of an organisation's daily operations and stakeholder interactions.

The leadership role

In values work every person is a leader. By virtue of our humanity and relatedness we all carry the responsibility for making values real. According to Rossouw[64], "Ethical leadership is thus not reserved to those in managerial positions.... Everyone in an organisation could be an ethical leader". Among other things, this leadership task is about leading with personal integrity and in the best interest of the organisation and doing so with honesty, fairness, respect, humaneness and courage.[65]

By embracing our potential for ethical agency, we add the yeast of values to the relational networks that we are a part of. Having said this, some among us also carry leadership responsibilities of a different kind. As the formal leaders of teams, departments or an organisation, they create the conditions and enable the processes for making values real. If you are in a position of formal leadership, you have several opportunities for values integration across a variety of interactions with the people you lead. Every interaction, whether a conversation, a meeting or other kind of event, is an opportunity for making values real. As a leader, you represent the value creation and values integration dimensions of your organisation's existence. Your task is to embrace, integrate and promote enterprise and community at the same time.

While I can refer to several aspects of the formal leadership task, I want to focus more narrowly on how you may utilise meetings as one of the best leverage points for organisational values integration. Why would I single out meetings? I do so because meetings represent communicative spaces where diverse voices on matters of common interest must be blended into decisions and actions that hold consequences for both the strategic direction and ethical character of an organisation. Meetings are where the relationship, and often the tension, between strategic, instrumental and communicative action becomes most real. It is in meetings that we often find that arguments and decisions in favour of strategic and operational expediency tend to overpower those that are values-driven and morally commendable. We can either see this tension as an unfortunate and inevitable trade-off or give values a chance of influencing the ethical quality of our decisions and actions. This is where values-driven leadership can make a difference. The question is how.

A few months after a values workshop, I had a debriefing interview with the head of a department. I was keen to know what values practices they were able to implement. Thankful for my interest she told me that she just came out of a most frustrating meeting. People were talking over one another, the loud voices dominated, and it was virtually impossible to come to a satisfying outcome. I asked her whether using an active listening approach in conversation pairs followed by reporting back on behalf of one another would have made a difference to the tone, inclusive participation by all, and the outcomes of the discussion. She admitted that it most probably would, if she only had thought about it when preparing for the meeting. Maybe she was caught on the wrong foot by thinking that it would be an easy conversation. From my perspective it would have been helpful if she'd prepared differently for leading the meeting.

Values are not made present just because we call them by name. Their presence emerges from how we go about our interactions and how we turn our conversations, even difficult ones, into values-driven decisions and actions. As a leader, whether in a smaller team environment or a more complex board level environment, you can prepare for it. The yeast of values remains at your disposal.

You can prepare for it by means of how you create and facilitate conversations in a meeting. Ask yourself several questions when you prepare for a meeting. How would you like participants to check in and create a relational and values-driven environment to set the tone for a meeting? To what extent does the meeting lend itself to asking participants to share what in their working environment, or in relation to the organisation in general, made them happy or angry in recent times? How can this sharing be combined with active listening in pairs and reporting back on behalf of one another? How can the feedback from these conversations influence the agenda of a meeting? Participants in the healthcare workshops carried these exercises over into their working environment, resulting in positive outcomes for their relationships, their interdisciplinary and inter-departmental collaboration, and conflict resolution.

Furthermore, should there be tough issues to deal with on a meeting's agenda, how can you use some of the tools presented in previous chapters to lead discussions towards values-driven outcomes? How can you use the Giving Voice to Values Canvas to prepare for a conversation of which you know beforehand will prompt rationalisations? While you should guard against abusing your leadership role in a manipulative way, consider how the canvas can be your guide for leading a conversation away from rationalised compromises toward values-driven arguments with ethical outcomes for the organisation and its stakeholders? In the appendix on page 150 you will find a step-wise description, based on the canvas of how this can be done.

In addition to the Giving Voice to Values Canvas, there is also the discussion guide based on the Competency Assessment of Responsible Leadership that you can use. Using CARL's five interconnected components, you may consider how a big issue on a meeting agenda can worked through to arrive at an ethical and actionable decision. I encourage you to revisit table 5.1 as well as the explanation in the appendix on page 149, of how CARL can be used in practice.

Using the processes, exercises and frameworks discussed in this book, and referred to above, will enable you to lead, what I call, norm-producing conversations. In difficult conversations not everyone starts on the same footing with having access to the same information, by applying the same values, and taking the same ethical stance on what should be done. If anything, these conversations most often amplify the tension between strategic and communicative action that I referred to before. Notwithstanding the variety of angles that people in a discussion might take on an issue under discussion, as leader you have the opportunity to guide meeting participants towards a new normative position that can be embraced by all concerned. In some cases, one discussion should be enough, while in others repeated conversations will have to happen over a longer period of time. For example, dealing with a reported issue of unethical conduct in your organisation should be dealt with as a matter of urgency while building an ethical culture will need consistent attention over time. Likewise, racism cannot be tolerated, but building an inclusive organisation is a process that must be constantly revisited. At the end of chapter 7, you will find a section on how norm-producing conversations can be facilitated.

Being a values-driven leader is about being and becoming, both for self and the people you lead. It applies in time and over time. It is about the person you aspire to be, the conditions you create, and the processes you apply to take others with you on the journey. Authenticity, in personal and organisational terms, is neither static nor a given, but built over time. It is not a condition at which we arrive, but a dynamic process that we have the opportunity and responsibility to keep working on within us and among us.[66]

The yeast of values can only work if kneaded into the dough of personal becoming and organisational culture formation. Over and above discipline and skill is this a reflective process that stays in touch with when knowing-in-action breaks down, when reflection-in-action is needed, and reflection-on-action is constantly refreshed. The good baker is both actively and reflectively engaged in the processes and outcomes of bread-making. We might even say that over and above using yeast, the good baker also becomes yeast. Similarly, values-driven leadership is about making values work as well as being the embodiment of values at work.

Conclusion

Can values be made to work in organisations? I have no doubt that it is possible, especially if we understand how the conditions conducive for working on this ideal can be created. By way of conclusion, and with the theory of the critical yeast in mind, I want to highlight three key messages that came through in this chapter.

Making values real in organisations is about giving the human and interpersonal nature of our existence the prominence that it deserves. There is no reason to believe that we should leave our humanity and relationality at the door when we enter organisational space. As human institutions, organisations exist for creating collective value beyond what individuals are able to do on their own. If we accept this premise, organisations are spaces of collaboration and co-production in which we participate as whole persons, our values included.

For an effective and ethical organisation, value creation and values integration are indispensably interconnected. The direction provided by the value creation process is complemented by the integrity that emerges from the values integration process. While working on this ideal does not guarantee an organisation without blemish or conflict, it builds and distributes ethical consciousness and competence across the organisation over time.

Having top leadership to set the tone and generate broad buy-in to increase the scope and speed of values integration is helpful but also come with caveats. It is better to work on the development of values-driven agency for all throughout the organisation and do what Tams and Gentile[67] refers to as the "facilitation of ethical voice". Achieving this goes beyond the mere possession of a set of espoused values. It involves making those values real where and whenever applicable in one conversation, one meeting, one decision at a time. Making values real is as much about having people who are serious about values, as about an organisation that systemically enhance the capacity and confidence of all its people to live and express those values.

The good baker knows that yeast is indispensable for turning flour and related ingredients into becoming bread, that yeast needs time to become ready to be used, and that proper kneading is essential for the yeast to do its work. So it is with values if we want their mediating capacity to ferment into the behaviours, relationships, decisions and actions in our organisations. How training and development can play a part in enhancing this process is the question that we'll pursue next.

The first step in every journey is often a matter of starting small. In my work with values I have found that organisational participants see potential for using and mastering one exercise at time. Assuming that you are involved in an organisation, use your reflection time to consider the questions below.

- How might the theory of the critical yeast help you to enhance your capacity for values integration in the organisational role(s) that you fulfil?
- Depending on your role(s) which of the exercises and instruments discussed and recommended in the book thus far would you like to try out in upcoming conversations or meetings?
- If you were to apply insights from this chapter to a more holistic approach to making values work in your organisation, where will you start? Whom will you most likely have your first conversation with?

CHAPTER 7

CULTIVATING VALUES THROUGH TRAINING

The concept of value education is a generic one that includes training in moral development, on the one hand, and training in competence development, on the other. — Milton Rokeach

INTRODUCTION

Right at the beginning of a values workshop a participant asked me whether values can be taught. He was prompted by his twin brother to ask me the question. His brother is a business ethicist, and he is an engineer. While the relationship between the two brothers is really coincidental to the situation, there is something very interesting in the disciplines they represent in relation to the question. On face value one may assume that the ethicist's interest comes from a more philosophical perspective and that of the engineer's from a more practical perspective. The ethicist may be more inclined to ask whether values can be taught and the engineer how such teaching can be effective. There might also be another - and perhaps more hidden - drive behind the question that connects the two brothers, namely that both of them have seen enough in life and business in practice to be sceptical about whether such teaching can make a lasting difference.

Our leading question, "How can we make values real?" now gets twisted into "How can training for making values real be done?" Asking the question in this way is not about avoiding the sting in the engineer's "can question" but about exploring it via the process orientation that we maintained since the beginning of the book. More specifically, the focus will be on the facilitation of training experiences through which participants can strengthen their ability for making values real.

Our journey through the chapter starts with some observations about the participants in values training initiatives. Thereafter follows an overview of the theoretical building blocks that I use for workshop design, the thematic flow of a typical values workshop, guidelines for workshop preparation, and the role of the facilitator. By way of closing, I offer a framework for the facilitation of difficult values-related conversations in which much of the preceding discussions will be integrated. As the reader you will notice how this framework integrates many of the processes and exercises referred to in earlier chapters into a facilitated norm-producing conversation with values-driven decision outcomes as its aim.

This chapter deals with the possibility that training can make a contribution to making values real. In all of what will be discussed, we remain connected to our central metaphor, namely adding value like a baker. We explore how people, through training, might become more knowledgeable, skilled and confident to work the yeast of values into their individual, relational, organisational and even citizenship practices.

The people factor in values training

Since my involvement in values work, I have presented bite-sized sessions in classrooms and webinars, whole modules as part of academic and management development programmes, training workshops within organisations ranging between a half day to two and a half days in length, and train-the-trainer workshops. Some of these occasions were once-off inputs and some formed part of long-term projects. For the discussion in this chapter, I do not want to deal with all these variations but narrow the focus down to a typical one-day training workshop facilitated with participants from the same organisation. Covering this, I have learned, provides enough of a basis for the design of other training applications.

Before attending to workshop design within an organisational context, I'd like to comment on the profile of people attending it. To start with, participants may be from the same or different organisational units. They may attend individually or as part of a group who decided to attend together. They may be from the same or different levels of seniority in the organisation. And, very importantly, they may be of similar or different language, cultural, ethnic, or religious backgrounds.

From a motivational perspective participants may represent a variety of expectations. Some will arrive with curiosity about what they can learn about values. Some will arrive because of desperation with their working conditions. Some may want to know how they can promote values in their areas of responsibility. Some are hoping for answers to difficult personal problems they are struggling with. I have also found that some may arrive without any specific expectations at all.

Lastly, participants do not arrive without values, but as people with experience of how challenging it at times can be to stay true to the values that are important to them. They know quite well about the yellow and red zone experiences involved in living their values. They arrive as real people with their stories of victory and stories of woundedness in their quest for making values real.

Understanding and respecting this "variety in presence" is important to keep in mind when considering the design and facilitation of a values workshop. Participants do not just represent a collective of attendees; they are individuals with unique stories and motivations becoming involved in a collective learning process with others. This learning process, whether they expect it beforehand or not, may become an existentially important experience for them. How this learning encounter with values will be play out for them matters a lot. Therefore, it needs to be carefully designed and sensitively facilitated.

The foundations of values workshop design

The ideal values workshop, I believe, should be a lived experience of what it means to make values real in practice. To say it the other way round, a workshop must equip participants to do in practice what they have learned, experienced and mastered in the workshop itself. Ideally, the learning process must be theoretically sound, personally empowering, and practically relevant.

There are four theoretical building blocks that inform my approach to values workshop design. They are all briefly discussed below.

Giving voice to values

Mary Gentile's work is fundamental for what it means and takes to make values real. Several references to her Giving Voice to Values (GVV) approach were already made in previous chapters. Here I want to highlight three principles that I adapted from what she describes as "an action-oriented curriculum for values-driven leadership"[68] for workshop design and facilitation.

Focus on action: When faced with a values conflict our challenge is mostly not about the awareness that it exists, nor the analysis of what is at stake. Our challenge is with taking the action that will resolve it effectively and ethically. At the heart of the learning process is not the transfer of new knowledge about values, but how such knowing translates into the development of confidence and competence for acting on them.

Work with possibility: Amid a values conflict it is more productive to ask what can be done than what should be done. The latter question narrows the options for problem-solving, while the former one invites the exploration of possibilities. Even if there is certainty in a values conflict about the right thing to be done, it still needs to be worked out in relation to other stakeholders and their roles, beliefs, interests – especially as expressed in rationalisations – and the conversations to be had with them. The learning process must be a living experience of this possibility orientation at the heart of which is a rescripting process.

Practice responsiveness: Mastering the practice of rescripting may lead to resolving values conflicts more confidently and competently over time. This is a skill that can be developed. The learning process should make this practice possible and encourage participants to make it habitual. This is not about practice guaranteeing perfection, but about practice that may increasingly deliver values-driven outcomes with all the benefits for personal integrity, relational well-being and organisational reputation that may result from it.

Gentile's GVV therefore sets the tone for workshop design by shifting the focus from a "learning about values" to a "practicing how to make values real" approach. The activities that bring this principle to life, will be explained in the next section of the chapter.

Theory of communicative action

In preceding chapters I have made several references to Jürgen Habermas' Theory of Communicative Action (TCA). I specifically highlighted his notion of interpersonal encounters as speech situations and the distinction he makes between strategic and instrumental rationality on the one hand and communicative rationality on the other. While Habermas' grand ideal with TCA was to restore dialogue and civic participation in the public sphere, I would like to highlight three key insights from his work that are particularly relevant to workshop design and facilitation:

Language and speech acts: According to Habermas[69], language serves to reproduce cultures and keep traditions alive, it makes social integration and the coordination of plans among different actors in social interaction possible and enables the cultural interpretation of needs. Through language we question, answer, address, object to or admit what is being exchanged between participants in a speech situation. He, furthermore, regards a speech situation as a process, a procedure and a product in which participants engage in argumentation without force or pressure to achieve morally valid outcomes.[70] In view of this, a values workshop can be regarded as a speech situation in which participants, on equal grounds, are enabled to both master the language of values and apply it to moral challenges in practice. I have often observed the empowering impact of values workshops on participants as they embrace the language of values and, through conversation with others, move towards new insights and actionable outcomes.

Communicative rationality: In previous chapters we explored Habermas' distinction between strategic and instrumental rationality on the one hand and communicative rationality on the other. Where the former dominates, factors such as authority, cost, expedience and short-term benefits tend to dominate decision outcomes. In communicative rationality participants strive to reach understanding based on consensus and under conditions that are free from force or pressure. Communicative rationality is, furthermore, built on the assumption that statements made by participants in a speech situation can be challenged and tested for being true, right and truthful.[71] It can therefore be argued that communicative rationality restores the rightful place of values and ethics as a valid source of truth next to the more measurable claims of strategic and instrumental rationality, for example financial statements, production outputs and sales numbers, in decision-making conversations. What we therefore by implication do in values training is to strengthen the ability of participants to integrate values into what might otherwise simply be regarded as "business as usual" conversations. This is important for the shift from rationalisations for not doing the right thing toward well-informed and morally based reasons for doing what is right. Considering the integration of values is therefore not merely an option but an imperative. Values, as we have claimed before, should ideally not be reserved for separate conversations, but are inherently present in every conversation.

Discourse ethics: This concept is well associated with Habermas and grew out of his TCA. We do not have the scope here to go into the detail of discourse ethics, except for explaining the conditions on which it is based. The first condition is that of universality and means that the interests of all affected by a discourse have been considered to such an extent that they can accept the outcomes, consequences and side effects thereof. In practical terms this refers to the fairness of a discursive process, for example, a decision and its outcomes. The second condition is that all participants in a discourse can approve of the norms that determined the outcomes thereof. In practical terms this refers to the validity of a discursive process. For a moral discourse to be fair and valid it needs to be inclusive of the interests and participation of all concerned and morally grounded and defensible at the same time.[72] What message does this hold for the design and facilitation of a values workshop? Previously, I referred to norm-producing conversations which – in discourse ethics terms – means that participants arrive communicatively and cooperatively at actionable values-driven decision outcomes. Ideally, a values workshop must mirror this process. At the end of the chapter, I discuss a framework for how such a conversation can be facilitated.

Altogether, Habermas' TCA restores the rightful place and integral role of values-driven considerations in everyday organisational speech situations where moral considerations have to be applied together with arguments informed by financial, technical or scientific considerations. The same applies where participants in a conversation might find themselves on different sides of a values conflict.

Theory U

Otto Scharmer[73] is renowned for his theory of change, generally referred to as Theory U. Diagrammatically it is usually illustrated as a U-shaped curve representing change as a process of letting go of the old and letting come of the new. While Scharmer's work represents a grand theory scalable to large systemic change processes with multiple actions, stages and stakeholders, we are here only interested in a small part thereof, namely, how to guide the learning process through a values workshop. Three concepts from Theory U are of relevance for our purposes, open mind, open heart and open will. These three concepts, in the way in which I make use of them for workshop design, help to build the journey of how participants enter, participate in, and commit to the outcomes of a workshop. How does this work?

Open mind and how we enter: People entering a values workshop arrive as individuals with different needs as described in the previous section. Depending on why they attend the workshop, they may know some other participants to some degree or may not know anybody else at all. Values also represent for many participants a very personal topic of discussion, especially if they are attending in the hope to resolve something really important to them. Taking this into consideration, it is important to create a hospitable context conducive to meeting others and being open for the kind of conversations and exercises to follow.

Open heart and how we participate: While making values real may be experienced as a very personal matter, the learning process is per definition a relationally embedded one. We learn values and uphold them in social processes of interaction. For a workshop it means that there should be a sufficient level of trust for participants to be open for sharing and taking part in activities that may for some be experienced as very personal. This is a facilitation imperative that should not be taken lightly.

Open will and how we commit: If we aim at equipping participants to be more confident and competent for making values real in practice, then a values workshop must enable them to let go of beliefs and actions that undermine their values-driven responsiveness and commit to new behaviours and actions that support it. From a facilitation perspective, one part of the process is to ensure that a workshop makes space for choice and commitment. The other part is to situate such choices and commitments in a context of communicative action where participants may also experience the support and encouragement of others. While strengthening participants' resolve, it also builds interpersonal accountability that improves the chances of making values real in practice.

In summary, Theory U helps with optimising the transformative potential of a workshop. Using this framework enables the facilitator to progressively deepen the learning journey for participants. They may enter as individuals but then discover that values are learned and nurtured through processes of socialisation. Eventually they also learn that for values to be real in practice require commitment to agency and action. The workshop is a vehicle for this process.

Myers-Briggs type indicator

You may be familiar with the Myers-Brigg Type Indicator (MBTI) (https://www.myersbriggs.org) as a personality assessment instrument based on preferences of how people perceive the world and make decisions. Among other things, the instrument is widely used for personal, team, and leadership development purposes. Here I do not intend to discuss the merits of the MBTI or the sixteen personality types that it has become known for. I merely want to point to the relevance of psychological preferences for how people prefer to learn. Taking cues from the MBTI, a workshop can be designed to cater for different personal learning preferences. I provide for these needs as described below.

- Providing for enough *theory, problem-solving and abstract thinking* will satisfy the learning needs of analytical, logical and conceptual learners.
- Providing *a supportive and collaborative learning environment* will satisfy intuitive, empathetic and imaginative learners.
- Providing for *structure and step-by-step guidance* will satisfy participants with a practical and detail-oriented learning style.
- Providing an *interactive and experiential environment* will satisfy participants with a preference for learning by doing and real-world applications.

Based on the MBTI one could say that designing a well-structured but interactive workshop that are theoretically and relationally satisfying improves the possibility of facilitating a learning process that every participant can enjoy. Such a process is practical, conceptually enriching, experiential, and meaningful. There is no reason why a values workshop cannot be serious and fun at the same time.

Based on the abovementioned four theoretical building blocks, an effective values workshop is a relationally embedded and communicative learning experience that builds the confidence and competence of participants for making values real in practice. With this ideal in mind, we can now attend to the actual process flow of the "standard" one-day workshop we are discussing.

Workshop content and process flow

There is always the risk that one may become too settled in the way you do things. However, taking the abovementioned theoretical building blocks into account, there is a structure and flow that I prefer to follow in the facilitation of a one-day values workshop. You may apply the same approach in designing your own or adapt as you deem necessary.

Session 1: Orientation

Even the start of a values workshop should go beyond the mere welcome and "who is who" type of introduction. I start a workshop by inviting participants to select someone as unknown to themselves as possible and then to have an active listening conversation with each other. The conversation may circle around three questions: Who are you? What do you do? Regarding values, what are you curious about? After about fifteen minutes, conversation partners introduce each other in plenary or in smaller groups depending on what is feasible in terms of the number of attendees. The mere act of active listening while building a relationship with another person and representing that person as truthfully as possible in feedback is already and exercise in making values real and it sets a relational tone for what follows in the rest of the workshop. It is also helpful to know what people are curious about so that those needs can be attended to in the conversations to follow.

It is also good to invite participants, right at the beginning, to participate at two levels, namely that which may evolve as common interests for discussion among the group as a whole and that which are of personal relevance to themselves. The topics and exercises that follow thereafter make both aims possible.

Session 2: What values mean and why they matter

The second session of the workshop starts with a happy - angry exercise, using the yellow and red cards as described in chapter 2 and comprehensively explained in the appendix on page 154. Once participants documented their yellow and red experiences we discuss the meaning of values as presented in the working definition used in this book, namely that values are aspirational beliefs that we hold about human behaviours expressing how we prefer or agree to live and relate and determining what we regard as right or wrong in particular situations and the decisions we make as a result.

Working together in small groups, participants get the opportunity to share their yellow and red zone stories and connect them to values either upheld or violated in these experiences. I usually work with the values of honesty, respect, responsibility, fairness and compassion. If participants have an existing set of organisational values, and if it is sufficiently useful for the purposes of the workshop, it can be used in a similar way. Another alternative is to work completely inductively and ask participants to discover the values at stake in their stories. Sharing the yellow and red zone stories sets the scene for a conversation about the link between emotions and values as discussed in chapter 3.

The last part of this session involves an exercise of meaning exploration in which each value is discussed in terms of what is means in practice, what difference it makes in upholding them and what difference it makes when neglected or violated. This work gets divided by assigning values to smaller working groups with feedback in plenary afterwards. It is in this exercise that participants experience the very practical nature of values as well as the interconnectedness among a broader collective of values. This exercise often reveals the gap that exists between an organisation's strategic and espoused formulation of values and participants' tacit experience thereof in practice.

Session 3: Values conflicts and the rationalisations for not addressing them

The tone of the conversation shifts in this part of the workshop. Whereas the previous section made the meaning of values tangible and practical, this one focusses on the reality of values conflicts. The notion of values conflicts is introduced to participants as an experience of values violation towards themselves, an observation of a values violation in the treatment of others, or as an awareness of behaviours or practices that may harm the organisation and its stakeholders. At this point the scene is set for Mary Gentile's thought experiment, A Tale of Two Stories. This exercise is done in silent reflection for about fifteen minutes during which participants document their two stories, one in which they experienced a values conflict and acted on their values, and another in which they did not act on their values. This reflection exercise is guided by the questions mentioned in chapter 3 as well as in explanation of the exercise in the appendix on page 143.

The reflection exercise is then followed by an active listening exercise. Active listening is firstly explained in more detail and then used to set up a safe space for sharing in conversation pairs. This sharing is not about the detail in the two stories, but about the difference in their outcomes as discovered through the reflective exercise. The feedback that follows in plenary is not about anything that was shared in confidence, but about what each listener learned from their conversation partner's account of the difference between acting vs not acting on values. This sharing usually turns into a serious conversation about speaking up versus shutting up and the experiences and repercussions of having done or not having done so. It usually provides for a vulnerable moment in the workshop as participants realise that they all share in the same human experiences.

On the Tale of Two Stories follows an explanation of GVV's four common rationalisations for not doing the right thing as discussed in chapter 3. These rationalisations are standard practice, materiality, locus of responsibility and locus of loyalty. Once the framework is understood, I invite participants to list, from their experience, examples of typical rationalisations that may be present in their organisation. The point of this discussion is not to make the organisation look bad, but to make the concept of rationalisations real. It is usually an enlightening moment for people to realise how pervasive the neglect and/or violation of values can become in an organisation.

Session 4: Rescripting for values-driven outcomes

Having dealt with rationalisations in the face of values conflicts the scene is set for a discussion about the meaning and practice of rescripting as discussed in chapter 4. Participants learn about the shift in focus from each of the four common rationalisations to rescripted values-driven alternatives. Once the necessary explanation is done, it is the ideal time for engaging in case study work. Working through a case brings the whole learning journey together. For working through a case study, I use the Giving Voice to Values Canvas and the questions that go with it as explained in chapter 4 and in the appendix on page 150. The questions guide the thinking process for the discussion while the canvas makes it possible to see everything on one page and work with the discussion in an iterative way.

You may wonder about where to find good cases to work with. A good case has at minimum a protagonist faced with a values conflict in relation to one or more other role players, there is evidence in the case of one or more rationalisations for not doing the right thing, and there is a question or statement in the case that signals the protagonist's uncertainty about how to get the right thing done.[74] For a starter you can find such cases on the Giving Voice to Values webpage of Darden Business Publishing. You can also look for good newspaper stories to work with. Some newspaper stories contain all the relevant attributes of a good case and may be contextually very relevant for a workshop group. Over time you may also develop your own case material, or you may ask, like I do, participants with good case examples to write their stories in a format that you can use for training purposes. In the case of gathering your own stories, it is important to get permission from the people you obtained them from and to protect their identity as well.

The main point of the case discussion is to make the practice of rescripting real for participants. Using the GVV Canvas with the case study allows participants to empathise with the protagonist by exploring their emotions, values, and the central conflict around acting versus inaction. Together with the protagonist they identify the rationalisations and work on rescripting towards a values-driven actionable outcome.

The debriefing that follows the discussion, provides more than just an opportunity for integrating the learning. Participants quite easily apply the insights they have gained to values conflicts that may occur in their own organisation. They also learn that a protagonist might experience a values conflict individually, but that dealing with it will most often have wider systemic implications. The story of George, the academic director that we discussed in chapter 4, is a good example of how systemically complex a values conflict and the rescripting process that follows from it might become.

This discussion can be closed by encouraging participants to apply the same process used in the case discussion to situations in their own lives, whether in private or at work. For this purpose, you may revisit the reflection exercise at the end of chapter 4. Time permitting, you can engage participants in a peer learning rescripting process around their own values conflicts or arrange or a follow-up workshop for attending to it.

Session 5: Values integration in practice

The concluding section in an organisational workshop is about ideas and actions for making the learning work in practice. The discussion is focused on how various elements of the workshop can be applied, amongst other uses, in conversations, meetings, decision making, stakeholder relations and contractual processes.

The leading question in this last session is what participants see as possibilities for making values real in their respective areas of influence and responsibility. To facilitate the conversation, I ask them to use green cards to write their ideas on. Once done they share, discuss and categorise their ideas. This inventory of ideas can be documented and used for post-workshop implementation and follow-up.

The use of green cards may be merely symbolic, but it is a helpful contrast to the yellow and red ones used at the beginning of the workshop. It stimulates thinking about what needs to be cultivated for making values real more consistently and habitually over time. I usually collect these ideas and write them up as a reminder of what participants envisioned as actionable outcomes. As a repository of ideas, it provides leverage for ongoing values work after the workshop as well as for lending support in specific areas of interest.

Through this last exercise I have found that participants spontaneously mention how the values under discussion got new meaning for them and how they feel better equipped to make them real individually as well as in interpersonal situations. They also mention how they are more mindful of values conflicts and better prepared to act on their values in such situations. Some also mention their intention to make values real in their general working environment and so also in meetings and decision-making processes.

Workshop preparations

In chapter 4, where I told the story about the healthcare project, I shared quite a lot about workshop preparations. The comments that follow are merely to systemise the most important aspects thereof.

Situation analysis

In the preceding section I described the flow of what may appear to be a "stock standard" one-day workshop within the same organisation. This, however, does not cancel the necessity of making a thorough situation analysis about whom the workshop is for and why there is a need for it. If it is by open invitation it is one thing, but if the workshop is requested by a specific group, it might influence your preparations, especially the choice of cases and exercises.

Composition of the training group

This is often an important conversation to have. It is about the choice between scale and depth. I have worked with groups over forty in size but prefer to cap numbers at 20. With larger groups you can generate more energy but sacrifice on the depth of learning. With smaller groups the depth of learning is better, but you reach fewer people at the same time. Some of my most meaningful workshops I had with between four and 10 people in attendance. Remember, in the end it is not about critical mass, but about critical yeast.

A discussion I often have with clients is whether management should go through a workshop first before other people in the organisation are exposed to it. If there is a good rationale for doing so, then let it be. In general, I prefer to compose training groups across the hierarchical layers of an organisation. The benefits of doing so were discussed in chapter 6 under the healthcare story.

Other than numbers there will be considerations about intra- versus interdepartmental group composition. Again, it is a matter of choice determined by the rationale for the training. However, from the healthcare case we have learned about benefits when people work across the divisional boundaries of an organisation.

Participant preparation

It is advisable to send a letter to participants about a week before a workshop. Use the letter to introduce the workshop, mention the schedule and themes, highlight the benefits of attending and attach reading material if necessary. Doing so, helps participants to attend with a positive expectation about the value of the training.

Venue and related arrangements

The venue room setup is not accidental but an essential part of your preparations. Avoid using numbers as the main criterium for the choice of venue. The venue must be appropriate for the activities you will be doing with a group. It must also be conducive for the communicative and relationally embedded nature of the learning process.

Avoid using a classroom or cinema type setup. With a programme group of 12 or less participants, a U-shape setup in combination with breakout spaces - in the same room - works well enough. When working with more than 12 participants, the interpersonal nature of the learning process determines the use of small group work. Small groups of between four and six participants work well.

It is best to limit the use of technology to the minimum. At most, I use a laptop and projector, augmented by flipcharts to capture discussions for feedback. Furthermore, I request participants to put all laptops and mobile phones away and only attend to emails and social media during breaks. As far as possible, participants should focus on their conversation partners and working groups and make the most of the relational and conversational experience and exercises of the learning process. Working with values, determine that participants take one another seriously throughout all the conversations and exercises of the learning process.

The role of the facilitator

You do not need to be a professional expert on values and ethics to facilitate a values workshop. However, there are few things that you should make a special effort of.

Become sufficiently knowledgeable: Familiarise yourself with sufficient of knowledge and insight about the topic so that you can facilitate a workshop with the necessary confidence and skill. Reading a book like this one, as well as others with similar content, can form part of your preparation. Also familiarise yourself with the organisation's values, code of ethics and/or conduct, policies that may have relevance for the topic, and professional and industry standards that may apply to the world of the participants.

Create a conducive environment: It is the facilitator's task to optimise the learning value for participants. This you can do by revisiting the four building blocks for workshop design that I described earlier in the chapter. Ask yourself how insights from Gentile's GVV, Habermas' TCA, Scharmer's Theory U and the MBTI can help you to design and facilitate a meaningful learning experience for the participants.

Don't teach, facilitate: Avoid the temptation to teach others about values. Rather focus on facilitating a meaningful learning process that will enhance their ability to make values real in practice. Be less occupied with what you can teach them and more interested in what you can learn together with them. As you move the learning process from one phase to the next, keep your focus on the conversations and exercises through which the learning becomes practical for them.

Guide through questions: Make a special effort of guiding the learning process through carefully crafted questions. Questions, especially ones that are open-ended, non-threatening and invitational, stimulate conversations and make exploration possible. Besides this, and especially as explored in chapter 4, asking the right questions is an important skill to master in values work. Let the workshop in itself be an example of how to work with questions that open conversations and build pathways towards solutions.

Apply helpful tools: The playbook in the appendix on page 143, has a description of all the exercises I have referred to in the book, and even more. My training pack usually contains packs of white, yellow, red and green cards, laminated A3-sized posters with the big five values on, copies of the case that I will using for the practice of rescripting, and four Jenga sets. There is not always enough time in a workshop for playing Jenga, but it helps to have it on hand when really needed. You find more information about using Jenga under the exercises included in the appendix on page 153.

Work toward actionable outcomes: It is important that participants leave the workshop with the belief that there is something that they can do to make values real. Therefore, make sure that the workshop ends with a discussion of actionable outcomes. In the one-day format you can at most conclude with the sharing of ideas for values integration in personal, relational and organisational process. In longer formats, there will be time available for participants to present their own situations and action plans with the GVV Canvas as a guideline.

Facilitating norm-producing conversations

Earlier I referred to the notion of norm-producing conversations. With this I am referring to participants involved in a conversation with moral consequences arriving communicatively and cooperatively at actionable values-driven decision outcomes. There is a sense in which this is the ideal that we strive for in all values conflicts, however small the scale of the interaction between the stakeholders might be. It is a different challenge, though, when a group wants to follow a values-driven approach with respect to larger issues with moral consequences. Here we can think, among other things, about topics such as transformation (including diversity, equity and inclusion) in the workplace, dealing with morally questionable business practices, working through ethical concerns around matters of performance, remuneration and wages, or what the organisation should do in terms of socially and environmentally responsible practices.

These "big ticket" items are seldom resolved in one conversation or workshop. Due to their systemic nature we have to work through them over time. We also know that merely following a strategic or instrumental action approach with these kinds of issues seldom lead to wholesome and sustainable outcomes in the long-term. How then can a values-driven facilitation approach, grounded in communicative rationality, help a group or organisation to have norm-producing conversations that advances progress over time. Below I explain the approach that I follow in this. The process contains a conversation through four stages and includes several of the elements and exercises that have been discussed throughout this book. You will also notice the influence of the GVV Canvas in the portrayal of the process. I have used this framework in facilitation a few times and it delivered promising outcomes.

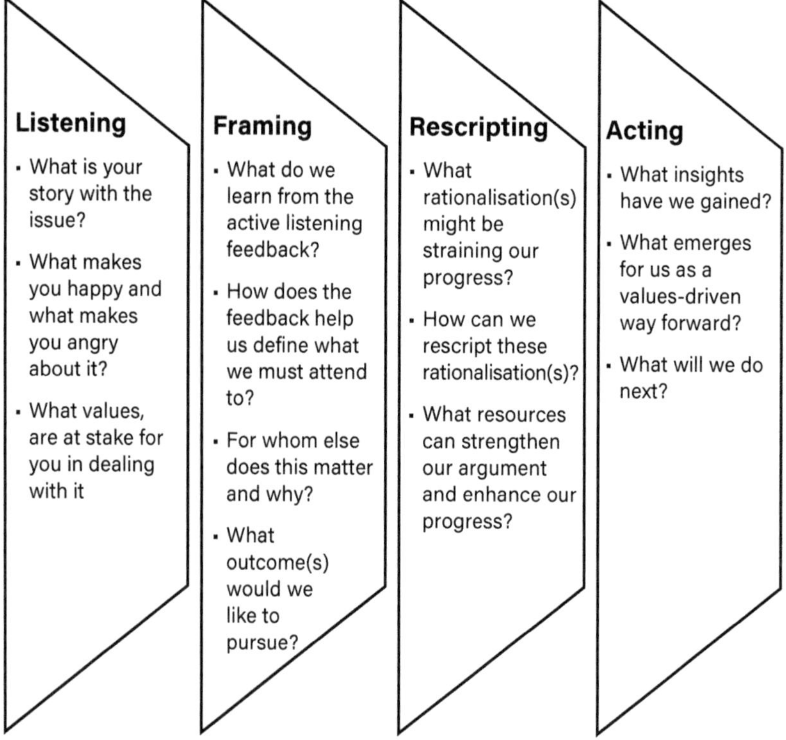

Figure 7.1: A framework for norm-producing conversations

As illustrated in the diagramme the process contains a listening, framing, rescripting and acting phase. The facilitation of these phases enfolds as described below.

Listening

Instead of starting on an argumentative foot in an open debate resulting in winners and losers, the conversation starts with an active listening exercise in which conversation pairs share their "stories" with the issue under discussion. Following the principles of active listening, conversation pairs use the opportunity to tap into each other's experience with the issue, and the emotions and values at stake for them. In the feedback that follows thereafter they share what they have learned about the issue from each other's perspectives. This approach makes inclusive participation in the discussion possible so that all voices can be heard irrespective of the differences in opinion, position or power among the participants. It democratises, so to speak, the conversation.

Framing

Depending on the size of the group, the feedback from the conversation pairs can be shared either in plenary or in working groups. Eventually all participants determine together what they are learning from the feedback to reach consensus about the issue under discussion. Based on this framing of the issue, they can explore the stakeholder context around the issue to determine who else might be affected by it or needs to be included in the ongoing conversation. At this point, having a better understanding of the issue and its repercussions, the group can determine their current position with respect to the issue and the outcomes that they would like to pursue for making progress with or resolving it.

Rescripting

Rationalisations do not only apply to individuals but to organisations as well. Rationalisations are often embedded in language, culture, traditions and organisational practices. It is important to identify these rationalisations that might be preventing change or straining progress with the issue under discussion. Rationalisations might be fuelled from standard practice considerations and based on arguments of how things have always been done. There is also the possibility that people in the organisation might try to minimise the material significance or risk of what is at stake around an issue. There could be rationalisations based on the argument that the problem sits elsewhere and is therefore not in the organisation's domain of responsibility to care about. Arguments could be raised about existing loyalties that may suffer or opportunities that may be lost as a result of taking a certain direction with an issue. Once identified, the rationalisations can be rescripted into values-driven reasons for doing the right thing. The rescripting work at stake might require research in various forms to be conducted. There could be the need to consult codes, policies, standards or regulations. The point is that this is a norm-producing communicative action approach aimed at building the best possible consensus-based argument for doing the right thing.

Acting

The last phase of the process is aimed at action and implementation. It is based on the same three questions contained in the GVV Canvas: What insights have we gained? What emerges for us as a values-driven way forward? What will we do next? Here is both reflection and action involved.

Responding to these questions may not be the final answer or result in a master plan for action. It may merely initiate the next step along a norm-producing pathway. Big issues are seldom resolved in one move. The whole process may need to be repeated with more stakeholder groups, or parts of the process may need to be revisited by the same group with whom the conversation started in the first place. Like the GVV Canvas, it is an iterative process.

Using this framework for more complex conversations emphasises again that making values real is not a quick fix but a long-term investment. A single intervention, for example, a workshop, can at most only be the beginning of a longer-term process if it is expected to have sustainable value, whether for individuals, teams or organisations. This kind of work is very personal and relationally and organisationally consequential at the same time.

Conclusion

Can values be taught? It is beyond our scope to go into the academic discourse among especially educators, philosophers and psychologists on the possibility of teaching values. Among these stakeholders in the conversation, we'll find a broad consensus that it is both possible and necessary, despite controversy on some of the issues at stake. The answer that we developed in this chapter points to a learning process through which people can become better at making their values explicit and apply it to resolving their values conflicts and ethical challenges in practice. Therefore, we twisted the question into the contribution that training can make in helping people to make values real more confidently, competently and consistently.

Considering whether values can be taught, we developed an answer that points towards the following:

- Strengthening the ability of individuals to act on their values holds positive benefits for the relational functional roles they play within an organisation and ultimately for the organisation as well.
- Growing this ability can best be done via a relationally embedded learning process in which participants grow in confidence to voice values, deal effectively with values conflicts, and integrate values across organisational processes, conversations, decisions and actions.
- A learning process through which this ideal can be accomplished must be theoretically and methodologically well-informed as well as practice-orientated.
- While participants in the learning process absorb new knowledge about values, they must also master new skills for making values real.
- The role of the facilitator is to create an enabling environment in which participants, individually and together, can be strengthened for making values real in practice.

Having stated the above, it remains to be said that making values real is a long-term investment. One values workshop, however uplifting, is but one yeast-adding moment in the life of an organisation. The process much be repeated and the reach thereof constantly extended to instil a fermentation process throughout an organisation. To become sustainable, it demands the discipline and attitude of a baker to work the yeast of values into the dough of organisational processes, practices and speech situations, day in and day out.

Consider your readiness to facilitate your first values training intervention. It does not need to be a full-length workshop. I may just be one exercise to start with. As preparation you can work through this chapter together with the references to other chapters within it. I recommend that you also consult the values playbook in the appendix on page 143.

In your planning consider the following:

- With whom would you like to do your first intervention?
- What is the situation that you would like to apply it to?
- What outcomes are you aiming for?
- What may your workshop design look like?
- What exercises would you like to try?
- What case study will you use?
- When will be the right time to do it?

CHAPTER 8

YES, WE CAN MAKE VALUES REAL

> The necessity of making moral ends wirklich (that is, real or actual) in the world, is a matter of morale, of confidence in the adequacy of our human potential.
>
> —*Mavis Biss*

We have come to the end of a journey in which we followed a question: How can we make values real? In reflecting on what we have learned, I briefly want to highlight four discoveries in response to the question and four practices for people who want to remain committed to this quest. Altogether they represent a summary of the book.

Four discoveries

Firstly, we discovered that making values real is *possible*. This is the case because values are part of who we are. Values are within us and among us. Yet, it is still a challenge to make them real consistently. We know it when we get it right and enjoy the benefits thereof. We know it when we get it wrong and suffer the consequences.

Secondly, making values real is a *process*. Sometimes a situation is such that we may almost inadvertently behave, decide or act in a values-driven way. Quite often the opposite is the case, and we may be faced with a values conflict that demands more careful considerations. We have discovered that help is available in the form of processes that we could follow to arrive at values-driven outcomes.

Thirdly, making values real requires *practice*. Several things in life require practice if we want to become adept in doing them. The same counts for values if we want to consistently experience the positive outcomes of making them real. This requires that we, for example, master rescripting as a practice in dealing with values conflicts. It also requires that we master a practice such as regular reflection to grow our moral consciousness and responsiveness.

Fourthly, making values real, is *proactive*. As individuals we can develop a proactive mindful orientation that improves our readiness for values-driven responsiveness across, whether in positive or confrontational situations. The same counts for our organisations when we grow a common vocabulary combined with agreements on how we go about integrating values-driven considerations into strategic and operational discussions.

Five practices

Looking back on the journey that we have followed, there seems to be five interrelated practices for people who take up the challenge of making values real. While these practices are for all values-driven people to pursue, they may be particularly relevant for those who lead in organisational roles. The practices are to make meaning of, voice, internalise, integrate and cultivate values. They are all interrelated as illustrated and discussed below.

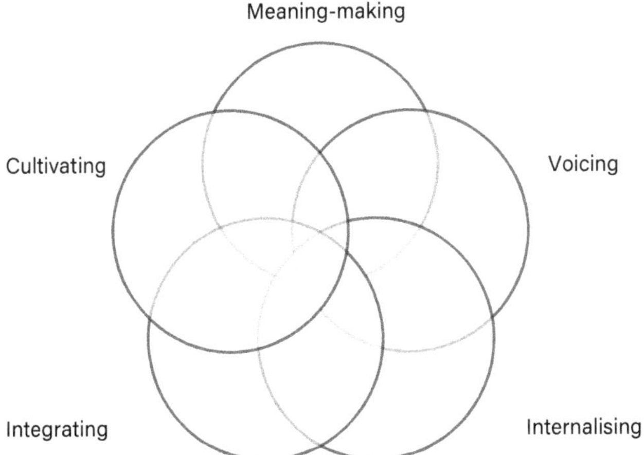

Figure 8.1: The practices of making values real

Meaning-making

The practice of meaning-making refers to ensuring conceptual clarity of what we mean when we refer to values. A blanket use of the concept leaves people with fuzziness and confusion. There are different kinds of values and there is a distinction between the things that we value and the ethical values that we have in common with others. We furthermore find that organisational values statements are mostly a mix of different kind of values. While there is a place for all of these expressions of value and values, our quest in this book was about ethical values. Following the process-based approach that I have advocated for from the beginning of the book, the task of meaning-making is about ensuring conceptual clarity in the first place and, secondly to enable people to deepen their understanding of the values they agreed to hold in common with others. In chapter 1 we worked on conceptual clarity and in chapter 2 we demonstrated, by means of five globally accepted values, how the process of meaning exploration can be done.

Voicing

The practice of voicing refers to ways of speaking and behaving when the values we hold are confronted by situations in practice. While we would like to assume that all values-driven people will stand their ground and speak their mind amid values conflicts, we know from experience that this is not the case. Circumstantial and relational factors, combined with personal consideration do play a role in whether or not people will voice their values in situations of confrontation. In the combination of chapters 3 and 4 we discovered that barriers to voicing our values can be overcome and that we can learn the skills and build the confidence and courage to do so. Understanding and mastering the practice of rescripting can make the voicing of our values easier and consistently more effective over time.

Internalising

The practice of internalising is both personal and relational. Values are personally embodied and relationally embedded. As a personal practice, it refers to what we do to build our own values-driven consciousness and competence. In chapter 5 we focused on the role that regular reflection can play in supporting this personal internalisation process. While reflection is helpful amid a values conflict, it works best when practiced as a regular discipline enriched by reading and journalling. On the relational side we also highlighted the importance of values conversations and peer coaching. These conversations provide valuable feedback and serve as relational networks that we can draw from in difficult situations. Internalising values, in personal terms and enriched by peers, helps us to build resilience for remaining on a values-driven pathway throughout our lives. We may not always succeed in getting the voicing of our values right, but it will help to have surplus reserves that we can always draw from.

Integrating

The practice of integrating, as we have discussed it in chapter 6, has primarily to do with organisations. If the big complaint is that organisations are not serious about practicing their espoused values, then we need to think about how it can be changed. This is a challenging task, one that is mostly caught up between competing rationalities in an organisation. The overriding temptation in organisations will mostly be to give free rein to strategic and instrumental rationality and only raise the need for communicative rationality when there is ethical trouble with reputational consequences in the air. Values integration in an organisation is about restoring the rightful place of communicative rationality and action in its behaviours, decisions and action. It is a hard task, but it can be done.

We have concluded that every values-driven individual can play a role, whether in personal, functional or leadership terms. The effectiveness of playing this role, however, hangs together with the mastery of the practice of meaning-making, voicing and internalising values as described above.

Cultivating

The practice of cultivating deals with the role that training can play in strengthening the consciousness, competence and commitment of people, especially organisational members, for making values real. In chapter 7 we explored in very practical terms how that can be done. There are requirements for making such training meaningful and effective. We may wish that such training can be purely based on information transfer and that the right knowledge will lead to the right behaviour, but evidence tells a different story. Values training, to be effective, is more like a cultivation process for which meaningful interventions need to be carefully designed if we wish to have satisfying and actionable results. We therefore explored the theoretical foundations for effective workshop design and stressed the importance of the training to be a lived experience of the making values real process itself.

Mind the gaps

Having read this book, you may be left with several questions. We have, for example, not dealt with the thorny issue of whistleblowing. We have also not gone into the question whether culture makes a difference in how people understand and practice their values. Nor did we touch on how artificial intelligence might eventually play a role in how we understand and practice values as human beings. We also need to think about making values real in the context of the climate crisis. And what about best practice examples of leaders and organisations who seems to have found effective and sustainable answers to the challenge of making values real? All these questions, and more, remain open. I hope that what is written, is enough food for thought for now.

The final word

The book's title suggests that making values real is akin to the working of yeast. In baking bread, the baker knows that the potential of the tastiest ingredients is dependent on adding the right amount of well-prepared yeast. Only upon preparing the right baking conditions and adding the yeast can the ingredients blend and rise and make the flavours burst. Yeast has become metaphorical of the difference that values can make in how we live, relate, work and lead. As we learn how to use values as yeast we also become better bakers of the conditions in which we and others can flourish as fellow human beings. Bread is life-giving, and so are values too.

APPENDIX: A VALUES PLAYBOOK

The variety of practical exercises we do in values workshops are all easy enough to be repeated in the workplace and other settings. I hold it as a matter of principle that whatever I do with participants in training must be repeatable by them when they return to their me-we-work-world domains of life.

I call this collection of exercises a "values playbook". It contains exercises stemming from Mary Gentile's Giving Voice to Values approach as well as exercises originating from other fields of application adapted by me and fellow facilitators for use in values workshops. Most of the exercises in this playbook have been referred to in different chapters of the book.

The aim of the playbook is to make the exercises we do in training workshops "portable" for use across various values-related situations. They are useful for building confidence and competence for making values real. They help us with putting the yeast of values to work. As we learn how to master this, values-driven living, relating and leading produce well-being for us as individuals, as teams, as organisations, and even as a society.

The exercises are alphabetically ordered. The situation will determine which exercise to use for what purposes, the combinations in which it may be used with other exercises, and how the outcomes of an exercise can be most meaningfully made use of.

A Tale of Two Stories

Much has already been written about this exercise as the cornerstone of Gentile's GVV framework. I include a short description of it having all the relevant exercises together in the same place. The version that I offer here is adapted from the complete description offered by Gentile self.[75]

I use the exercise as an introduction to the discussion of values conflicts. The first part of the exercise is of a reflective nature. Participants work on two worksheets respectively covering an experience in which they acted on their values and one in which they did not. The two scenarios, together the reflective questions that go with each, are presented as follows:

- **Scenario 1:** Recall a time in your work experience when your values conflicted with what you were expected to do. You spoke up or acted to resolve the conflict. What was the situation? Who else was involved? What did you say or do? What motivated you to speak up or act? How satisfied were you with the outcome? What would have made it easier for you to speak up or act?
- **Scenario 2:** Recall a time in your work experience when your values conflicted with what you were expected to do. You did not speak up or act to resolve the conflict. What was the situation? Who else was involved? What motivated you to not speak up or act? How satisfied were you with the outcome? What would have made it easier for you to speak up or act?

The second part of the exercise is an active listening conversation among conversation partners following the pattern as described in chapter 7 (see the section referring to the third session in a one-day workshop). The third part is a plenary discussion delving into the speaking up versus shutting up conundrum that participants are so often confronted with.

This is an exercised not to be missed in a values workshop. On the one hand, it is liberating for people to share their battles with values conflict. On the other hand, it brings perspective on the reasons why people so often choose not to take up and do something about a values conflict.

Time permitting, I often follow the Tale of Two Stories with the "I am conflict" exercise in this playbook.

Active listening

Active listening can used to help people master the skill of listening attentively and respectfully to another and represent that person's views to others. It can be used in combination with, for example, the happy vs angry exercise, the Tale of Two Stories, appreciative inquiry interviews, and the GVV Canvas when used in peer coaching. While being a very helpful exercise, active listening can also be regarded as a habit to be developed and a demonstration of values in action.

As a very versatile practice, active listening can be used for various purposes, for example,

- at the beginning of a meeting for checking in, even among people who regularly work together
- at the beginning of a workshop for participants to getting to know and introducing one another
- for creating safe conversation spaces for people to discuss a sensitive topic
- for getting multiple perspectives on a situation or topic under discussion, especially when it is necessary to give all participants a chance to make a contribution in peer coaching around a rescripting exercise.

To set it up, the facilitator asks participants to form conversation pairs and give them one or more questions to interview each other about and explain to them what is required for feedback. It is important to encourage participants, especially in a sensitive conversation, to listen carefully and respectfully to what the other has to say, to probe for better understanding, to suspend judgment and refrain from any advice-giving. When regrouping, ask the conversation pairs to represent each other's views. This can either be done in plenary or in small groups depending on how many people there are in the meeting or workshop.

While the exercise offers a non-judgemental setting for individuals to voice what they think, feel or experience in a particular situation it also helps a group of people to appreciate the multiplicity of experiences or views that are present among them. Instead of defending their own positions or arguments, it liberates them to explore alternative perspectives on an issue under discussion. It benefits the engagement of all by transcending the boundaries of experience, rank and power so that all voices can be heard. It helps to democratise the conversation space.

Appreciative inquiry interviews

Appreciative inquiry is a positive psychology and strengths-based approach to organisational change and development.[76] The methodology includes an interview in which participants focus on capacity, potential and aspiration in a situation of problem-solving. It steers conversations away from the downward spiral of problem analysis and focuses the energy on solutions.

Appreciative inquiry can be used in a problem-solving context where the leading question is not about "why something is the case", but "how it might be best resolved". It can also be used to explore the value of a particular concept or idea, for example, values-driven leadership, or the practising of one or more shared values, or for ideation around values-related workplace issues such as transformation, performance management, or people well-being.

Similar to active listening the exercise is based on conversation pairs that report back to a plenary session directly or indirectly via working groups. The exercise takes the form of an active listening interview based on four generic questions. The questions are related to high-point experiences that participants had about the topic under discussion, aspects that they value about themselves in relation to the topic, the core factors in relation to the topic that give life to the organisation, and the ideals the interview participants have about their contributions to a positive future for the organisation. In chapter 5, I explained how this interview format can be applied to the ideation of values-driven leadership in practice.

When facilitating the exercise, it is best to print the question sheets and give a copy to each participant for use in the conversation pairs. Participants are encouraged to make notes so that they can represent each other faithfully in the feedback to working groups or in plenary.

Depending on the time available, the interview part of the exercise can be about 30 minutes in length. Feedback can be directly to plenary or via working groups. Participants share that which they found most inspiring from interviewing their conversation partners. The task of the facilitator is to move the conversation to a place where participants may find common ground around ideals which can be translated into action plans.

Case discussions

The use of a case from elsewhere may help participants to gain insight into something that they need to deal with themselves. In values training, a case discussion creates the opportunity to practise multiple values concepts and skills at once, for example, when used in combination with the Giving Voice to Values Canvas. It can also be used, for example, when a group may have a values conflict that is too sensitive to confront directly.

Case discussions are especially useful for seeing the relationship between an issue, usually represented by a protagonist, other stakeholders and their needs and interests and a broader organisational or societal context. In a values conflict, a case discussion can throw light on rationalisations and help participants to imagine what effective rescripting might look like.

In setting up a case discussion the facilitator's first task is to determine whether this kind of exercise will benefit the achievement of the preferred outcomes in a particular situation, for example, a values conflict. The second task is to find a suitable case to discuss. Reference was made in chapter 7 to where cases can be found. In values training the instructions for a case discussion can be combined with the use of the Giving Voice to Values Canvas and the questions that go with it.

Clear instructions enhance meaningful feedback conversations, whether the case under discussion is part of a training workshop or another kind of meeting. Irrespective of how a conversation was structured (all participants together in plenary, or among groups of two or more participants), there may be different interpretations of what the essence of the case is about, the rationalisations that may be held by key stakeholders and the rescripting that may be most helpful. This enriches the learning experience.

An essential aspect of a case discussion is to allow discussion time for the integration of what has been learned and the consequences thereof for personal, team or organisational practices.

Circles in the air

This exercise is adapted from The Climate Change Playbook.[77] The exercise illustrates how perspective affects the way we see things and the actions that we take on the basis thereof.

How does it work? Participants are instructed to raise their right arms straight above their heads and with their index fingers pointing towards the ceiling as in the illustration on the right.[78] Next they are instructed to swing their arms in big circles in a clockwise direction, while keeping their eyes on the tip of their stretched-out index fingers. Once they get the feel of the movement, they are instructed to bring the movement downwards by bending their elbow while keeping their forearms still straight upwards and keeping the focus on their index fingers. When everybody's index fingers are about at eye level, the movement can be stopped, and participants are asked what they observed in the process. What really happens in this exercise is that the movement that is observed as clockwise when the arm is fully stretched out upwards is seen as anti-clockwise when the index finger is lowered to match eye-level. It often takes some time before someone comes up with the correct answer and the facilitator can repeat the exercise until all participants get the point.

In a values workshop, this adaptation of the exercise works well to illustrate the relationship and tension between strategic rationality (referring to the enterprise-related dimensions) on the one hand and communicative rationality (referring to the community and relational dimensions) on the other in organisations. It fits very well at the beginning of the organisational values integration discussion in a values workshop (in other words, just before session 5 in the workshop structure as explained in chapter 7). The upwards circular movement symbolises strategic rationality and is premised on the ever greater and faster achievement of measurable results, for example, sales, customers, profits, and dividends. The horisontal eye-level circular movement symbolises communicative rationality and is premised on seeing and appreciating the people and values involved in the value creation process. The organisation is enterprise and community at the same time. To be effective and ethical, value creation and values integration are two complementary perspectives on the same movement. An organisation needs them to be in harmony, but quite often they are in tension. When in tension, the risk is to allow the expedient nature of strategic and instrumental rationality (the upwards stretching circles) to override the consensus seeking nature of communicative rationality (the horisontal eye-level circles). This is an experiential and embodied exercise that generates a lot of amazement and fun among participants. It is also an exercise that they tend to remember for long afterwards.

Competency Assessment of Responsible Leadership (CARL)

This exercise has been comprehensively discussed in chapter 5, especially in relation to its potential for mastering reflection and values-driven problem-solving. Recommendations for how to make personal use of it were also provided in the reflection section at the end of chapter 5.

What remains here is to encourage you to use it in training workshops as well. This is how I make use of it:

- Once I have decided on using CARL for teaching or training, I send the link (https://carl2030.org/) with the necessary instructions to participants together with a deadline on when they must complete it. I also request that they bring their feedback report to the class session or workshop.
- In the case of an academic programme, I often combine the use of the instrument with a written reflective assignment based on the questions listed in the third column of table 5.1. In the case a normal workshop, I will just use it as a basis for discussion and problem-solving.
- The first round of engagement with the CARL feedback is focused on understanding the instrument and its personal application. Thereafter I put participants in discussion groups to share what they have learned from their feedback and how they plan to make use of it.

Degree of mastery (columns) Competency dimensions (rows)	**Knowing (Knowledge)**	**Doing (Skills)**	**Being (Attitudes)**
Stakeholder relations	2	3	2
Ethics and values	3	3	2
Self-awareness	4	2	2
Systems understanding	3	2	3
Change and innovation	3	4	2

Illustration of CARL results[79]

In the second round of engagement with CARL, I prefer to use a case study, specifically selected to fit the context of the group that I am working with. Such a case, I normally get from online news articles. The case conversation is built on questions similar to those listed in fourth column of table 5.1. Quite often I will build a role play into this discussion as illustrated by the loan application case in chapter 5.

This exercise taps well into several of the key dimensions of making values real by using reflection to build personal values consciousness as well as group-based problem-solving on the basis of a communicative action approach towards consensus building and decision making.

Giving Voice to Values Canvas

The Giving Voice to Values Canvas, as illustrated in chapter 4, represents an integrated map for working through a values conflict. It can be used to help individuals, teams and even a whole organisation to become more systematic, skilful and confident in working through values conflicts.

The canvas is normally introduced and practised in a training context where it is ideal for working systematically through a case discussion. The canvas can also provide the framework for the discussion of a complex organisational issue as discussed at the end of chapter 7. Once understood, individuals can use the canvas when they need to work through a personal values conflict. A mentor or coach with knowledge of the canvas can also use it to help individuals and teams to work through their values conflicts.

In discussing a values conflict, whether represented by a case discussion or based on a personal or team-based situation, it is important to 1) bring participants in touch with their emotions; 2) identify the values-confrontation at stake; 3) work through the me-we-work-world consequences of speaking up or not; 4) identify the rationalisations that prevent action; 5) identify alternative scripts for action, and 6) decide on helpful first steps to be taken. Working through the canvas helps people to navigate the thinking-feeling-doing disjointedness that comes with a values conflict and to find helpful ways towards authentic re-scripted responses, whether in terms of what they say or do.

Happy - angry exercise

The exercise is used to help people explore the feelings they have about a situation. These feelings often reveal the values that matter most to them. While happy feelings often relate to values being upheld in a situation, angry feelings may point to values being compromised or violated.

The exercise works well in a training workshop to help people identify the values that are important to them or understand why they experience known values to be either upheld or violated. In a team context, the exercise can be used to evaluate the extent to which shared values are practised in the context of their daily activities and relationships.

To do the exercise participants are provided with A6-sized yellow and red cards on which they write their happy (yellow) and angry (red) experiences. Participants can write as many happy and angry experiences as they like as long as they write only one per A6 sheet of paper. Depending on who the participants are the instruction for writing these experiences can include life experiences in general or more narrowly focused on the workplace. Participants are given about ten minutes to write their happy and angry experiences on the colour-coded sheets.

Once done, the experiences are shared, and similar ones are collated and categorised. I have previously described how value can either be extracted from the experiences or how experiences can be related to existing values, for example, the five values discussed in chapter 2 or the shared values of an organisation. In values training the exercise helps participants to explore the relationship between values and emotions and especially the relationship between angry emotions and values conflicts. This exercise, specifically in the way in which it reveals angry feelings, forms an ideal introduction to the Tale of Two Stories exercise through which the difference between acting vs not acting on values is explored.

I am conflict

This exercise has not been discussed in any of the book's chapters. However, its use is very similar to the "circles in the air" exercise, namely, to allow people an embodied learning experience. In the case of "I am conflict", participants are invited to explore their instinctive reaction towards dealing with conflicts in general and then relate that to how they tend to respond to values conflicts. I often use this exercise after the Tale of Two Stories in a training workshop.

The exercise works well in a sufficiently large space, inside or outside, where people can move around in response to the instruction they are about to receive. The exercise starts with the participants gathering randomly around the facilitator. The facilitator then announces her or himself as "I am conflict" and instructs participants to "Take an embodied position that expresses your feelings towards me". It is interesting to note how some participants move as far away as possible, even turning their backs, how some come close up, how some remain where they are, but with folded arms, etcetera. While participants remain in their positions, the facilitator then identifies some and invites the group to discuss what they observe about a person's embodied position and attitude regarding conflict and what the benefits or disadvantages thereof could be. Those participants who were identified for discussion are also invited to share their views on the positions that they have taken.

While there is not necessarily a direct relationship between how we handle conflicts in general in comparison with values conflicts, most people seem to associate with the possibility that it is the case for them. By doing this exercise we have another angle on what we experience and how we tend to respond amid a values conflict. It leaves participants with much food for reflective thought.

Jenga

Jenga is a game that many people are familiar with. It involves a tower of wooden block perpendicularly layered in levels of three blocks each. Players take turns to take blocks from below the topmost completed layer to build the tower upward until it falls over. It can be played in one group or in teams depending on the number of participants involved.

The game is preceded by the explanation of the rules, namely, 1) to build the tower higher up with blocks available in the tower; 2) to first complete a layer before moving to the next; 3) to only play with one hand; 4) to be only allowed three attempts to find a block to take and place it on top, 5) not to try to reconstruct the tower as a block is placed, and 6) that every participant must take part.

Jenga can be played in one group or with several teams at the same time. In the case of only one group the game continues until the tower topples. The loser is the person who causes the tower to fall. In the case of many groups playing simultaneously, I place a time limit of 15 minutes on the game and the winning group is the one with the highest tower when time is called.

Why use Jenga in values training? Firstly, it is very much akin to the "circles in the air" exercise by demonstrating the tension involved in achieving a predetermined goal in a values-driven way. At the same time, it illustrates the tension between the rules of the game and the commitment of the participants to play it in a values-driven manner. In debriefing the exercise, the discussion can be about the extent to which the participants succeeded to express the values of honesty (sticking to the rules), respect (allowing each to play irrespective of skill), responsibility (foreseeing the consequences of how a block is played an placed), fairness (ensuring that all groups and all individual players are judged by the same standards) and compassion (no judgement in the case that someone makes the tower topple and the team needs to start all over again).

The debriefing can also involve a discussion of processes, e.g., planning (how to approach the game), communication (sharing and listening to insights or perspectives from others), decision-making (what blocks to play and how to place them), patterns of stuckness (repeating the same action over and over, for example, playing only middle blocks), and risk-taking or avoidance (in terms of increasing the height of the tower). In the debriefing it is especially the connection between the practising of the values and the processes at play in the dynamics among the players that matters most.

Values exploration

The values exploration exercise forms the basis of what has been discussed in chapter 2 of the book. The exercise enables participants to explore the meaning of values in view of three questions: What does the value mean for us in practice? What do we gain from practicing the value? What results from neglecting or violating the value? Depending on the purpose of the exercise, a fourth question can be added: How can the practice of this value be strengthened?

I prefer using sticky boards and coloured A6-sized paper sheets to facilitate this exercise. Contributions to meaning are written on white, while yellow is used for upholding a value and red for neglecting or violating it. Green is used for strengthening the practice of a value. In the absence of sticky boards sticky notes on flipcharts sheets can work equally well. Ideally, there should be a sticky board or flipchart in the room for each

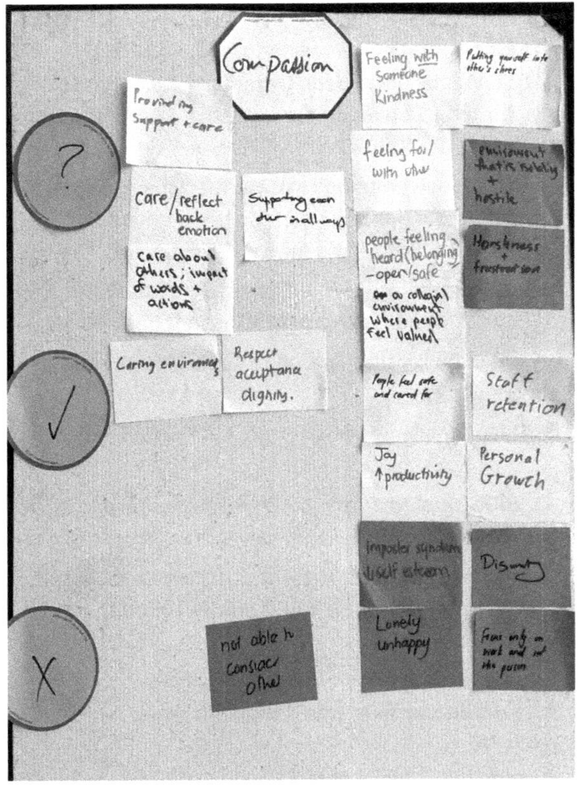

value under discussion. Once all the contributions are posted, the work is divided among smaller groups to categorise and theme all the contributions for feedback and discussion in plenary.

The point of the doing the exercise in this way is that if offers every participant the opportunity to contribute to the meaning-making process. It brings, so to speak, the values within practical reach of every participant. What so often is experienced as philosophically fuzzy or strategically distant from organisational participants, become real for them.

BIBLIOGRAPHY

Auster, ER & Freeman, RE. 2013. Values and Poetic Organizations: Beyond Value Fit Toward Values Through Conversation. *Journal of Business Ethics* 113(1):39–49. https://doi.org/10.1007/s10551-012-1279-5.

Bagozzi, RP. 2003. Positive and negative emotions in organizations, in *Positive organizational scholarship: Foundations of a new discipline,* edited by KS Cameron, JE. Dutton, & RE Quinn. Berrett-Koehler Publishers, Inc.:176–193.

Biss, M. 2014. Moral Imagination, Perception, and Judgment. *The Southern Journal of Philosophy* 52(1):1–21. https://doi.org/10.1111/sjp.12050.

Buber, M. 2011. *I and Thou.* A translation with a prologue 'I and You' and notes by Walter Kaufmann. Kindle edition.

Competency Assessment for Responsible Leadership. nd. CARL2030. https://carl2030.org/.

Cooperrider, D & Whitney, D. 2005. *Appreciative inquiry: A positive revolution in change.* San Francisco, CA: Berrett-Koehler Publishers, Inc. (Kindle edition).

Crane, A, & Matten, D. 2007. Business ethics, in *The A to Z of Corporate Social Responsibility*, edited by W Visser, D Matten, M Pohl, & N Tolhurst. John Wiley & Sons, Ltd.:52–59.

Darden Business Publishing. nd. *Business Case Studies & Business Publications.* https://store.darden.virginia.edu/WidgetsBrowse/categoryNew?categoryId=716.

De Déa Roglio, K. & Light, G. 2009. Executive MBA programs: The development of the reflective executive. *Academy of Management Learning & Education* 8(2):156–173.

Edgar, A. 2006. *Habermas: the key concepts.* London New York, NY: Routledge, Taylor & Francis Group (Kindle edition).

Frederickson, BL. 2003. Positive emotions and upward spirals in organizations, in *Positive organizational scholarship: Foundations of a new discipline. Edited by* KS Cameron, JE Dutton, & RE Quinn. San Francisco: Berrett-Koehler Publishers, Inc.:163–175.

Freeman, RE & Auster, ER. 2011. Values, authenticity, and responsible leadership. *Journal of Business Ethics* 98(1):15–23. https://doi.org/10.1007/s10551-011-1022-7.

Freeman, RE & Auster, ER. 2015. *Bridging the values gap: How authentic organizations bring values to life.* Oakland, CA: Berrett-Koehler Publishers, Inc.

Gentile, MC. 2010a. *Giving voice to values: How to speak your mind when you know what's right.* New Haven, USA: Yale University Press (Kindle edition).

Gentile, MC. 2010b. Keeping Your Colleagues Honest. *Harvard Business Review* 88(3):114–117.

Gentile, MC. 2010c. Turning Values into Action. *Stanford Social Innovation Review* 8(4):43–47.

Gentile, MC. 2011. Giving voice to values: An action-oriented curriculum for values-driven leadership. *EFMD Global Focus* 5(1):34–38.

Gentile, MC. 2014. Giving voice to values in the workplace: a practical approach to building moral competence, in *Ethics training in action: an examination of issues, techniques, and development,* edited by LE Sekerka. Charlotte, NC: Information Age Publishing:164 –182.

Gentile, MC, Lawrence, AT & Melnyk, J. 2015. What Is a Giving Voice to Values Case? *Case Research Journal* 35(2):1–10.

Groenewald, L & Dondé, G. 2017. *Ethics and compliance handbook.* Pretoria: The Ethics Institute.

Habermas, J. 1984. *The theory of communicative action, Volume 1: Reason and the rationalization of society.* Translated by T McCarthy. Cambridge, UK: Polity Press. (Kindle edition)

Habermas, J. 1987. *The theory of communicative action, Volume 2: The critique of functionalist reason.* Translated by T McCarthy. Cambridge, UK: Polity Press. (Kindle edition)

Habermas, J. 1990. *Moral consciousness and communicative action.* Translated by C Lenhardt and SW Nicholsen. Cambridge: MIT Press (Kindle edition).

Health Professions Council of South Africa. 2021. *Guidelines for practice in the healthcare professions: General ethical guidelines for the healthcare professions.* https://www.hpcsa.co.za/Uploads/professional_practice/ethics/Booklet_1_Guidelines_for_Good_Practice_vDec_2021.pdf

Institute of Directors in South Africa. 2016. *King IV report on corporate governance for South Africa 2016.*

Institute of Directors in South Africa. 2016. *King IV Report on Corporate Governance for South Africa 2016.* https://www.iodsa.co.za/global_engine/download.aspx?fileid=3EFA955E-5F1F-4031-88F2-979C2BF100F6

Lederach, JP. 2005. *The moral imagination: The art and soul of building peace.* Oxford: Oxford University Press (Kindle edition)

Maak, T & Pless, NM. 2006. Responsible leadership in a stakeholder society: A relational perspective. *Journal of Business Ethics* 66(1):90–115. https://doi.org/10.1007/s10551-006-9047-z.

Meadows, DL, Sweeney, LB and Martin-Mehers, G. 2016. *The climate change playbook: 22 systems thinking games for more effective communication about climate change.* White River Junction, Vermont: Chelsea Green Publishing (Kindle edition)

Merriam-Webster. 2023. Ethos. In *Merriam-Webster.com Dictionary.* Merriam-Webster Inc. https://www.merriam-webster.com/dictionary/ethos

Merriam-Webster. 2023. Ethics. In *Merriam-Webster.com Dictionary*. Merriam-Webster Inc. https://www.merriam-webster.com/dictionary/ethics

Mintz, SM. 1996. Aristotelian virtue and business ethics education. *Journal of Business Ethics* 15(8): 827–838.

Myers & Briggs Foundation. nd. https://www.myersbriggs.org/.

North, ZM, Smit, AT, & Jenkins, LS. 2022. A values-driven approach to vaccine hesitancy conversations. *South African Family Practice* 64(1):1–4. https://doi.org/10.4102/SAFP.V64I1.5419

Park, N, & Peterson, CM. 2003. Virtues and organisations, in *Positive organisational scholarship: Foundations of a new discipline,* edited by KS Cameron, JE Dutton, & RE Quinn. San Francisco: Berrett-Koehler Publishers, Inc.:33–47.

Parker, P, Wasserman, I, Kram, KE, & Hall, DT. 2015. A relational communication approach to peer coaching. *The Journal of Applied Behavioral Science* 51(2):231–252. https://doi.org/10.1177/0021886315573270.

Plump, C. 2019. How Giving Voice to Values Can Transform a Toxic Workplace Culture. *People and Strategy* 42(3), 40–45.

Rokeach, M. 1973. *The nature of human values*. New York: The Free Press.

Rokeach, M. 1979. *Understanding human values: Individual and societal*. New York: The Free Press (Kindle edition).

Rossouw, D. 2023. *Ethical leadership handbook*. The Ethics Institute.

Rossouw, D, & Van Vuuren, L. 2017. *Business Ethics*. 6th edition. Cape Town: Oxford University Press Southern Africa.

Republic of South Africa. 1996. *Constitution of the Republic of South Africa [No. 108 of 1996]. 38*. https://www.gov.za/sites/default/files/images/a108-96.pdf

Scarantino, A, & de Sousa, R. 2021. Emotion, in *The Stanford Encyclopedia of Philosophy*, edited by EN Zalta. Metaphysics Research Lab, Stanford University. https://plato.stanford.edu/archives/sum2021/entries/emotion/

Rubin, RS & Riggio, RE. 2005. The role of emotional intelligence in ethical decision making at work, in *Positive psychology in business ethics and corporate responsibility*, edited by RA Giacalone, CL Jurkiewicz, and C Dunn. Greenwich, Connecticut: Information Age Publishing:191–209.

Scharmer, CO. 2009. *Theory U: Leading from the future as it emerges*. San Francisco, CA: Berrett-Koehler Publishers, Inc.

Schoeman, C. 2014. *Ethics can: Managing workplace ethics*. Randburg: Knowres Publishing.

Tams, C & Gentile, M. 2020. Giving voice to values: responsible management as facilitation of ethical voice, in *Research Handbook of Responsible Management*, edited by O Laasch, D Jamali, Freeman, RE & R Suddaby. Cheltenham: Edward Elgar:532–548.

The Practo Blog for Doctors. 2015. *The Hippocratic Oath: The Original and Revised Version.* https://doctors.practo.com/the-hippocratic-oath-the-original-and-revised-version/

United Nations. 1948. *Universal declaration of human rights*. United Nations; United Nations. https://www.un.org/sites/un2.un.org/files/2021/03/udhr.pdf

Spataro, SE and Bloch, J. 2018. "Can You Repeat That?" Teaching Active Listening in Management Education. *Journal of Management Education* 42(2):168–198. https://doi.org/10.1177/1052562917748696.

The Ethics Institute. nd. https://www.tei.org.za/publications/.

The World Medical Association. 2017. *Declaration of Geneva*. https://www.wma.net/policies-post/wma-declaration-of-geneva/.

Vivier, E, Robinson, B, Jenkins, L & Smit, A. 2024. Institutional logics and relational shifts: Permeating hierarchies and silos in the healthcare sector. *Public Management Review* 26(10):2943–2965. https://doi.org/10.1080/14719037.2023.2299929.

Werhane, PH. 1998. Moral Imagination and the Search for Ethical Decision-Making in Management. Business Ethics Quarterly:75–98.

ENDNOTES

1 Rokeach, 1979:2.
2 Rokeach, 1979:48.
3 Gentile, 2010a: location 741.
4 Freeman & Auster, 2015:19–26.
5 Rossouw & Van Vuuren, 2017:8.
6 Groenewald & Dondé, 2017:10–13.
7 United Nations, 1948.
8 Republic of South Africa,1996: section 7–39.
9 Institute of Directors in South Africa, 2016:43–44.
10 Merriam-Webster Dictionary, 2023.
11 Crane & Matten, 2007:52–59.
12 Rossouw & Van Vuuren, 2017:5.
13 Mintz, 1996:828–829.
14 Park & Peterson, 2003:34–47.
15 Schoeman, 2014:8.
16 Freeman & Auster, 2015:49.
17 Gentile, 2010a: location 704–952.
18 Freeman & Auster, 2015:18–22.
19 Gentile, 2010a: location 129.
20 Scarantino & de Sousa, 2021:1.
21 Scarantino & de Sousa, 2021:48.
22 Frederickson, 2003:164–168.
23 Bagozzi, 2003:182.
24 Rokeach, 1973:7.
25 Gentile, 2010a: location 964–1235.
26 Gentile's, 2010a: location 128.
27 Gentile, 2010a: location 2431.
28 Rokeach, 1973:13.
29 Gentile, 2010a: location 128.
30 Gentile, 2010a: location 2373.
31 North, Smit & Jenkins, 2022.
32 North, Smit & Jenkins, 2022.
33 Plump, 2019:43.
34 Rubin & Riggio's, 2005:10.
35 De Déa Roglio & Light, 2009:157.
36 De Déa Roglio & Light, 2009.
37 Schön's, 1983.
38 Gentile, 2010b.
39 Gentile,, 2010c.
40 Maak & Pless, 2006:99.
41 Maak & Pless, 2006:105.
42 Competency Assessment of Responsible Leadership, nd.

43 Habermas, 1984:285–286.
44 Edgar, 2006:79.
45 Habermas 1990: location 106.
46 Spataro & Bloch, 2018:168.
47 Cooperrider & Whitney, 2005.
48 Parker, Wasserman, & Hall, 2015.
49 Gentile, 2010a: location 3206.
50 Biss, 2014:8.
51 Lederach, 2005: viii.
52 Werhane, 1998:85.
53 Gentile 2010a: location 346.
54 Rossouw & Van Vuuren, 2017:8.
55 Freeman & Auster, 2015.
56 Rossouw & Van Vuuren, 2017:127–141.
57 Gentile, 2014.
58 John Paul Lederach, 2005:87–100.
59 The Practo Blog for Doctors, 2015.
60 Physician's Pledge of the World Medical Association, 2017.
61 Health Professional Council of South Africa, 2021.
62 Vivier, Robinson, Jenkins, & Smit, 2024:2961.
63 Buber, 2011:62.
64 Rossouw, 2023:1.
65 Rossouw 2023:6–13.
66 Freeman & Auster, 2011; Auster & Freeman, 2013.
67 Tams & Gentile, 2020.
68 Gentile, 2011.
69 Habermas, 1990:25.
70 Habermas, 1984:25–26.
71 Habermas, 1984:99.
72 Habermas, 1990:65–66.
73 Scharmer, 2009.
74 Gentile, Lawrence & Melnyk, 2015.
75 Gentile, 2010a: location 964–1235.
76 Cooperrider & Whitney, 2005.
77 Meadows, Sweeney & Martin-Mehers, 2016:56–61.
78 Meadows, Sweeney & Martin-Mehers, 2016:56.
79 Competency Assessment for Responsible Leadership, nd.

INDEX

W

Y

www.ingramcontent.com/pod-product-compliance
Ingram Content Group UK Ltd.
Pitfield, Milton Keynes, MK11 3LW, UK
UKHW020142250726
13967UKWH00002B/810

9 781991 272256